P9-DNE-739

Praise for Math Puzzles and Brainteasers

Terry Stickels combines his masterful ability to create diverse, challenging and just plain fun puzzles with a wide range of math concepts, in a playful way that encourages the solver to discover their own unique methods of finding solutions.

—**David Kalvitis**, author of *The Greatest Dot-to-Dot Books in the World*

Logical, numerical, spatial/visual, and creative thinking problems can all be found within these covers, embracing a wide spectrum of thinking skills for developing minds. Terry Stickels also encourages indulgence in mathematical play, which for young students is an indispensable component of motivated and successful problem solving.

—**Barry R. Clarke**, *Mind Gym* compiler, *The Daily Telegraph* (UK)

Even kids who are not math nerds will enjoy this book. Stickels hits the perfect mix of brainteasers: They're challenging while still managing to be great fun at the same time!

—**Casey Shaw**, Creative Director, *USA WEEKEND* magazine

Terry Stickels is clearly this country's Puzzle Laureate. He has concocted a delightful and challenging volume of brainteasers that belong in every math teacher's library. Focused specifically on grades 3–5 and grades 6–8, these puzzles both educate and sharpen children's critical thinking skills. As an award-winning puzzle constructor myself, I am always in awe of what Terry comes up with.

—**Sam Bellotto Jr.**, Crossdown

Jossey-Bass Teacher

Jossey-Bass Teacher provides educators with practical knowledge and tools to create a positive and lifelong impact on student learning. We offer classroom-tested and research-based teaching resources for a variety of grade levels and subject areas. Whether you are an aspiring, new, or veteran teacher, we want to help you make every teaching day your best.

From ready-to-use classroom activities to the latest teaching framework, our value-packed books provide insightful, practical, and comprehensive materials on the topics that matter most to K–12 teachers. We hope to become your trusted source for the best ideas from the most experienced and respected experts in the field.

MATH PUZZLES
and
BRAINTEASERS,
Grades 3–5

Over 300 Puzzles that Teach
Math and Problem-Solving Skills

Terry Stickels

JB JOSSEY-BASS
A Wiley Imprint
www.josseybass.com

Published by Jossey-Bass

A Wiley Imprint

989 Market Street, San Francisco, CA 94103-1741—www.josseybass.com

No part of this publication may be reproduced, stored in a retrieval system, or transmitted in any form or by any means, electronic, mechanical, photocopying, recording, scanning, or otherwise, except as permitted under Section 107 or 108 of the 1976 United States Copyright Act, without either the prior written permission of the publisher, or authorization through payment of the appropriate per-copy fee to the Copyright Clearance Center, Inc., 222 Rosewood Drive, Danvers, MA 01923, 978-750-8400, fax 978-646-8600, or on the Web at www. copyright.com. Requests to the publisher for permission should be addressed to the Permissions Department, John Wiley & Sons, Inc., 111 River Street, Hoboken, NJ 07030, 201-748-6011, fax 201-748-6008, or online at www.wiley.com/go/permissions.

Permission is given for individual classroom teachers to reproduce the pages and illustrations for classroom use. Reproduction of these materials for an entire school system is strictly forbidden.

Readers should be aware that Internet Web sites offered as citations and/or sources for further information may have changed or disappeared between the time this was written and when it is read.

Limit of Liability/Disclaimer of Warranty: While the publisher and author have used their best efforts in preparing this book, they make no representations or warranties with respect to the accuracy or completeness of the contents of this book and specifically disclaim any implied warranties of merchantability or fitness for a particular purpose. No warranty may be created or extended by sales representatives or written sales materials. The advice and strategies contained herein may not be suitable for your situation. You should consult with a professional where appropriate. Neither the publisher nor author shall be liable for any loss of profit or any other commercial damages, including but not limited to special, incidental, consequential, or other damages.

Jossey-Bass books and products are available through most bookstores. To contact Jossey-Bass directly call our Customer Care Department within the U.S. at 800-956-7739, outside the U.S. at 317-572-3986, or fax 317-572-4002.

Jossey-Bass also publishes its books in a variety of electronic formats. Some content that appears in print may not be available in electronic books.

Printed in the United States of America

ISBN: 978-0-4702-2719-0

FIRST EDITION

PB Printing   10 9 8 7 6 5

Contents

Contents

Foreword

One of the advantages of growing up in a large extended family is that on numerous occasions I have had the opportunity to observe a miraculous transformation: A young, helpless, and ignorant epsilon—as the mathematician Paul Erdos called young children—comes into the world, begins to eat, drink, cry, dirty his or her diapers, grow (and grow and grow), and, last but not least, assimilate and process information about the world around this new being. Somewhere around the age of three that child becomes a genius.

The idea that all children for a short while in their lives are geniuses has been put forth in both humorous and serious ways by pundits and quipsters galore. The imaginations of children at this young age are unfettered, their preconceptions virtually nonexistent. The names "Plato" and "Socrates," which appeared on ear tags of stuffed animals of a granddaughter of mine, immediately became "Playdough" and "Soccer-team." After all, who were these strange Greeks who were impinging on her sovereign right to name her own animals? The animals still would recognize their names, wouldn't they?

A daughter of mine once politely refused an offering of sauerkraut at a neighbor's dinner table, saying that she didn't like "sourcrap." Another time I found one of my children blithely sitting in an empty laundry basket counting—or at least trying to count—the hundreds of square holes in its sides. The sole purpose of the endeavor apparently was to get some up close and personal information about the basket.

These personal recollections are not intended to impress the readers of this book with the cleverness or cuteness of my own progeny. Everyone who has raised a child or who is growing up will have story after story of their own. Some of these stories will be more humorous than those given here, some will show more intelligence on the part of the children involved, some will reveal unexpected turns of kindness, and some will parody the imperfections and mannerisms of the child's parents. The point is that in the life of every child is a period when that child is highly creative, unassuming, and, in my opinion, highly intelligent. Children look at the world through a pair of magical glasses, wired to, and designed to program the most complicated computer in the world, the human brain.

Then something goes terribly awry. Children gradually become larger physically, a bit more mature mentally, and we set about formally socializing and educating them. They lose their magical glasses and naiveté, and many of the educational processes to which we subject them seem to take on the form of a mass forced-feeding. But then, amazingly, a dozen or so years down the line, we begin to hear comments to the effect that the true geniuses among us, the truly creative people in our midst, are the ones who, for reasons that no one quite understands, have not lost their magical glasses, have not become fully educated in a sense. These elite thinkers are the ones who still see the world—even if it is an adult world they now see—through the eyes of a child.

What has happened to most children in our educational systems, in modern parlance, is a failure to communicate. To be sure, part of this failure is necessary. No new educational theory, no new process or program, no new technological process (at least presently available) will negate all of the negative aspects of having to introduce so much information to so many children in what of necessity has to be a highly organized, almost regimented, manner. But we don't have to throw all of the babies out with the bathwater. We can attempt to fight back.

Enter Terry Stickels and this book. It is a book intended to stem the loss of creativity in the educational process, grades 3 through 5, particularly in mathematics. Mr. Stickels is a highly successful and well-known creator of puzzles, one of the best we have in the country at this time. We need to only casually look at the quantity and variety of puzzles he has created to realize that he is one of those people who has a strong creative force permanently embedded and dispersed within them. He has for certain not lost that childlike ability to look at the world in new ways—and on a daily basis at that. His *FRAME GAME* puzzles, for example—some of which appear in this book—remind me of the way that children create words like "playdough" for "Plato" and "sourcrap" for "sauerkraut." He is the only adult I know who I believe could compete with children in this regard. And that is a compliment. He has spent a lot of time and energy writing this book and has consulted with various knowledgeable experts concerning the mathematical content.

Advice is given elsewhere on how to use this book, but I would like to throw in my two cents' worth also. If you are a child reading this Foreword, send Mr. Stickels an e-mail and ask him to write a more advanced book for you. If you are a teacher, a parent, or a friend of a child in the appropriate age group, go ahead and browse, browse, browse. Pick problems that pique your curiosity, ones that turn you on. You will find many. Choose ones that concern the topic of interest at the moment. You will find several. Present these to the children you are concerned with as challenges—challenges to have fun with. Do not present many at once. Even one is sufficient sometimes. And finally, be patient, very patient. Don't always expect success.

Based on my own experiences in mathematics, I can tell you with certainty that an incorrect analysis of one puzzle, if only you will hang onto your thoughts, might well prove to be the key to solving another one, and actually might well make you appear to be a genius at some later time. No one has to know that most of your thinking came from an unsuccessful attempt with another puzzle!

Getting this idea across to people in general, and to young people in particular, is difficult. But an old cliché in sports does a fairly good job of doing this: It's not whether you win or lose that counts, but how you play the game. The follow-up, in intellectual matters especially, is that how you play the game determines how many games you win in the future.

Again, it merits pointing out that, judging from my contacts with him and the impression he gives of being a workaholic, Terry Stickels has invested an enormous amount of time, physical labor, and highly skilled creative thinking in producing this book. More so than perhaps we realize. Based on numerous conversations with him, I can vouch for the fact he passionately cares about the American educational system. Let's give the gentleman a chance to do what he can with the puzzles he presents here. Here's hoping that this is not the last publication we see from him concerning the training of our young people in mathematics.

February 2009   Dr. Harvy Baker
                                          Department of Mathematics
                                     University of Texas at Arlington

Acknowledgments

This book would not have been possible without the work and suggestions of the following people:

Mr. Sam Bellotto Jr. of *CROSSDOWN.COM*

Ms. Terry Baughan of *TALLROSE PRODUCTIONS*

Ms. Shelley Hazard of *PUZZLERSPARADISE.COM*

Mr. Barry Finnen of *PHYSICS247.COM*

Webmaster Mr. Roger Smith

Mr. Robert Webb of *SOFTWARE3D.COM*

Ms. Suzanne Alejandre of *THE MATH FORUM@DREXEL*

Mr. Martin Gardner

Mr. Casey Shaw of *USA WEEKEND* magazine

Mr. Brendan Burford of *KING FEATURES*

Ms. Kelsey Flower

Mr. Alex Stickels

Finally—a special thanks to my right hand and the person who makes all this happen, Ms. Christy Davis, owner of Executive Services, Arlington, Texas.

About This Book

Puzzles and brainteasers are fun ways to get kids enjoying and thinking about math. The "thinking smart" puzzles in this book are designed to sharpen the creativity and problem-solving skills, as well as the mathematics content skills, of students in grades 3 through 5.

The design for the book includes the following objectives:

- Offer a panoramic approach to the thinking skills that kids need to excel in math

- Incorporate a broad spectrum of different kinds of puzzles

- Meet the grade-appropriate guidelines set forth by the National Council of Teachers of Mathematics

- Venture into content areas where previous math/thinking skills books have not gone

- Be challenging, but also offer lots of fun along the way

The puzzles are easy, medium, and difficult, but none are so designated. What one student will find easy, another may find difficult, and vice versa. A difficulty rating also might be intimidating to some students—and interpreted as a good reason for *not* solving a puzzle—the opposite of the book's purpose.

The range of puzzles incorporates multiple approaches to skill building, including numerical manipulation, spatial/visual problems, and language arts exercises. There is no one "best" pathway to solving each puzzle, and often there are numerous entry points to finding solutions. Students invariably will find the way, using a mix of intuition and thinking skills that are uniquely their own.

The Author

Terry Stickels is dedicated to helping people improve their mental flexibility and creative problem-solving capabilities through puzzles—and making it fun. His books, calendars, card decks, and newspaper columns are filled with clever and challenging exercises that stretch the minds of even the best thinkers. And he especially enjoys creating puzzles for kids.

Terry is well known for his internationally syndicated columns. *FRAME GAMES*, appearing in *USA WEEKEND* magazine, is read by more than 48 million people in six hundred newspapers weekly. *STICKELERS*, published daily by King Features, appears in several of the largest newspapers in America, including the *Washington Post*, the *Chicago-Sun Times*, and the *Seattle Post-Intelligencer*. Terry is also the featured puzzle columnist for *The Guardian* in London—the United Kingdom's largest newspaper.

As a highly popular public speaker, Terry's keynote addresses are fast-paced, humorous looks at the ability (and sometimes the lack thereof) to think clearly. Distinguished authorities such as the National Council of Teachers of Mathematics also praise his work as important in assisting students to learn how to think critically and sharpen their problem-solving skills.

Born and raised in Omaha, Nebraska, Terry was given his first puzzle book at age eleven. Fascinated by the book's mind-bending playfulness, he soon was inventing puzzles on his own—lots of them. He attended the University of Nebraska at Omaha on a football scholarship, and while he was at UNO tutoring students in math and physics, he saw the advantages of using puzzles to turbocharge understanding of several concepts within those disciplines.

After several years as an occasionally published creator of puzzles, Terry was asked to produce a weekly column for a twelve-newspaper syndicate in Rochester, New York. Two years later, his puzzles caught the attention of Sterling Publishing in New York, and his first book, *MINDSTRETCHING PUZZLES,* became an immediate hit and is selling well to this day. Twenty-five more puzzle books have followed, three of them sponsored by the high-IQ society MENSA.

Terry lives in Fort Worth, Texas, where he is working on his next generation of puzzles to once again captivate, challenge, and delight his worldwide readership.

Introduction

This book contains more than 300 puzzles, ranging from relatively easy logic challenges to more difficult math brainteasers, requiring math skills ranging from addition and subtraction to determining probability and algebraic thinking. Within these pages you will find these types of puzzles:

Mathematical	Frame Games
Spatial/Visual	Cryptograms
Logical	Analogies
Analytical Reasoning	Sequence
Word Puzzles	Sudoku

By design I have included a large number and broad spectrum of puzzles, providing teachers and learners with multiple options. These are organized into parts devoted to numbers and operations; geometry and measurement; mathematical reasoning; and algebra, statistics, and probability. This arrangement will facilitate the instructor's ability to enhance areas of the curriculum that are most appropriate, adding richness, change of pace, and reinforcement to the teaching/learning process.

Some Puzzle-Solving Tips

Puzzle solving is sometimes like mathematical problem solving, but sometimes you have to move away from the more standard approaches when working on puzzles. Think about the puzzles from different perspectives and with a sense of play. Consider some of the following:

- Can the puzzle be solved by breaking it down into simpler components?

- Are there patterns that repeat often enough to suggest a prediction for "what comes next"?

- A puzzle may have one or more answers.

- Try thinking of ways to "twist, bend, separate, or spin" the puzzle. What does it look like "backward, forward, upside down, and sideways"?

- Does your answer make sense? Can you plug your answer back into the question to satisfy all the parameters?

- If your answer seems strange or unlikely, it may well be correct. The answers to puzzles are often surprising!

- Don't worry about how you might be seen if you can't solve the puzzle. We all make mistakes, and no one can answer every question. Just relax, have a good time, and never worry about other people's opinions.

Projects throughout the book marked with a ✋ symbol can be done using easy-to-find manipulatives, such as coins, blocks, and cut paper, to help learners who may have trouble visualizing some of the puzzles.

You may wonder why some language arts puzzles are included in a math puzzle book. Actually, puzzles and problems such as analogies and analytical reasoning that are more "language arts" in nature promote and augment critical-thinking skills. Take the *FRAME GAMES*, for example. *FRAME GAMES* are words, letters, pictures, fonts, and the like, juxtaposed in a way to reveal a common idiom, famous person, athlete, movie, song title, and similar things. These include components of spatial/visual thinking, language, memory, vocabulary, and lighthearted fun. When people solve even one puzzle correctly—and find the fun in doing so—they are eager to jump to the next challenge, even if it is a puzzle of a different kind. Also, solving a type of puzzle in one area often triggers the mind into a flexible mode that makes it easier to solve problems/puzzles in other areas.

Another appealing feature of the *FRAME GAMES* is that they don't always follow the standard left-to-right or top-to-bottom pattern for their solutions. Mental flexibility from different perspectives is required. These puzzles can be used in a broad spectrum of classroom situations—from special education to warm-ups in calculus classes. They are placed periodically throughout the book, offering both a mental break and a different type of thinking challenge.

There is no wrong way to use these puzzles. They're meant to be treated like a good watch or pair of shoes: to be used over and over again. And they never wear out!

Here are some application ideas:

- As warm-ups to introduce a new element of math curriculum
- As a focus for competition among teams
- As an inspiration for learners to create their own versions to share with classmates
- Featured on posters or class newsletters as the puzzle of the day, week, month, or holiday

- For group problem-solving exercises
- Sent home for sharing with friends and family
- As the basis for discussions on how certain puzzles might have real-life applications and how they might be used within various professions
- Chosen randomly, just for fun!

The options are endless, as the marriage of mathematics and puzzle solving continues to be a winning combination to achieve new levels of accomplishment in elementary school classrooms everywhere. And that, in turn, contributes to developing lifelong learners who enjoy all aspects of the thinking process, as miraculous and ephemeral as it sometimes can be. I'm reminded of the introduction to Martin Gardner's book, *AHA! INSIGHT*,* where the following appears:

> *Exactly what goes on in a creative person's mind when he or she has a valuable hunch? The truth is nobody knows. It is some kind of mysterious process that no one has so far been able to teach to, or store in, a computer.*

---

*Martin Gardner, *AHA! INSIGHT,* Washington, D.C.: Mathematical Association of America, 2006. Copyright © Martin Gardner, 2006.

$$\pentagon + \pentagon + \triangle + \triangle = \underline{\quad 38 \quad}$$

Part 1

$$\begin{array}{r} TWO \\ +\,TWO \\ \hline FOUR \end{array}$$

NUMBERS
and
OPERATIONS

 $7\frac{1}{4}$

$L \times I \times = ?$

Whole Numbers

1. What is the next number in the sequence below?

   49

   1   4   9   16   25   36   _?_

2. Place the numbers 1–12 in the twelve circles below so the sum of each side of the triangle is 36. I will give you a head start by placing some of the numbers for you. (The numbers may be used once only.)

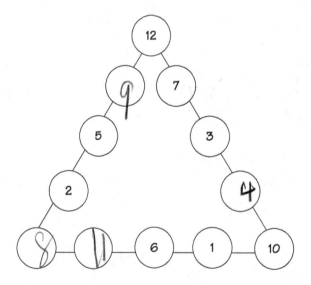

Copyright © 2009 by John Wiley & Sons, Inc.

3. My brother has a summer job and earns $5 an hour. He is going to work 5 hours a day for 5 days a week, and will do this for 5 total weeks.

a. How much money will he make in 1 week?

125

b. What is the total amount of money that he will earn?

625

4. Brenda bought a new catcher's mitt for $75. Her mom saw another mitt that was a better quality glove and cost less, so she bought it for $60. Brenda sold her first mitt for $65. A week later, Brenda's mom accidentally threw her new glove in the trash. Brenda found her first mitt for sale a month later for $50. She bought it back. How much money did Brenda and her mom end up losing on these transactions?

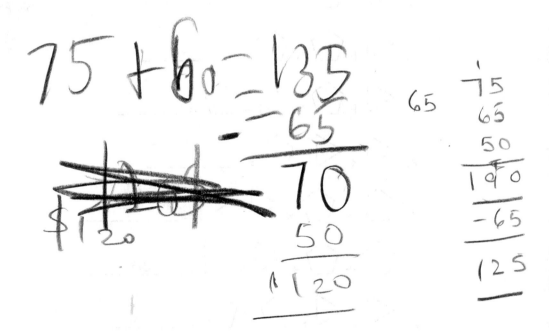

Copyright © 2009 by John Wiley & Sons, Inc.

5. Two shapes are each given a value. Each value is a whole number. This whole number is at least 0 and at the most 10.

◁ + ⬠ = 19   ◁ > ⬠   ⬠ = 9

Write the value for the following shape.

◁ = 10

Once you know the value, do the following exercises by replacing the shape with its value.

a. ⬠ + ◁ = 19

b. ◁ + ⬠ × ◁ = 100

c. ◁ + ⬠ × ⬠ = 91

d. ◁ + ⬠ × ◁ - ⬠ = 91

e. ◁ × ◁ - ⬠ = 91

f. ⬠ + ⬠ × ◁ - ◁ = 90

g. ⬠ + ⬠ + ◁ + ◁ = 38

h. ◁ + ◁ + ⬠ × ⬠ = 101

i. ◁ × ◁ × ⬠ + ⬠ = 909

j. ◁ + ⬠ × ⬠ + ◁ = 101

HINT
Remember the order of operations. Two of them are done for you.

Copyright © 2009 by John Wiley & Sons, Inc.

Copyright © 2009 by John Wiley & Sons, Inc.

6. Mrs. Johnson was going to purchase an iPod on sale for $250. At the checkout counter she received an additional 10% discount. How much did Mrs. Johnson pay for the iPod after the discount?

225

7. In the addition problem below, the digits B and C represent a number different from any of the other numbers shown (that is, not 1, 4, 5, 6, or 9).

```
 B5
+C9
164
```

$b = 8$ $6 = 7$

What are the only two possible values for B and C?

8×7

8. What is the missing number in the pie below?

85
79
164

$? - 6$

9. The grid below has a certain pattern to it that holds true for each row. Can you determine that pattern and find the missing number?

6	3	8
4	9	6
7	5	5
9	3	7
8?	8	4

HINT #2
What operations might be involved?

HINT #1
The first two numbers might determine the third number.

10. Can you determine the missing number in the box? The same rule of logic applies to all three boxes.

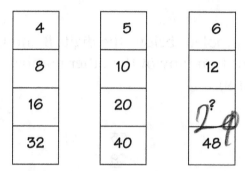

4	5	6
8	10	12
16	20	2? 24
32	40	48

11. The three numbers in each box have a relationship that is the same in all six boxes. Knowing this, can you find the missing number where the question mark is? What is the relationship?

3 2 7	1 5 6
4 0 8	4 3 5
10 1 1	6 2 ? 4

Copyright © 2009 by John Wiley & Sons, Inc.

12. In the addition problem below, the letters AB represent a two-digit number. If you know that the letter B is not a zero (0), can you tell me which numbers represent A and B?

65

```
 AB
 AB
+AB
───
19B
```

HINT
There is only one number besides zero that B could be. What is it? Why?

13. Below is a fun puzzle called an alphametic. Each letter stands for a different digit. Zero (0) is sometimes used for alphametics, but it can never start a word. You may use any of the digits 0–9.

```
  TWO
+ TWO
─────
 FOUR
```

This puzzle has only one solution if we let the letter W = 2 and R = 6. Can you find the other numbers that fit the addition problem?

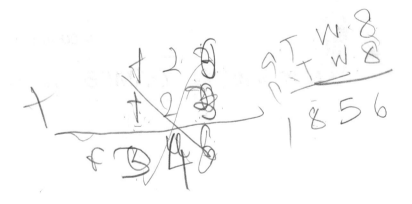

Copyright © 2009 by John Wiley & Sons, Inc.

Just for Fun: Frame Game

14. Find the hidden phrase or title.

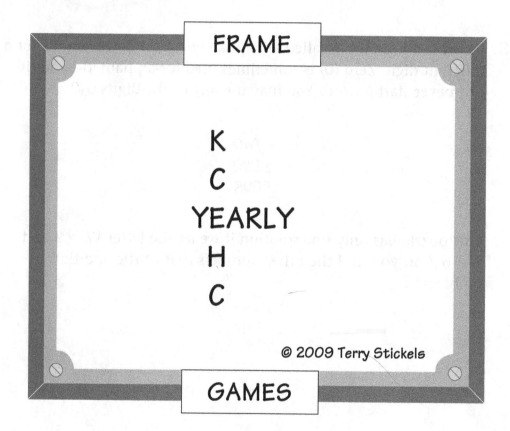

15. Analogy puzzles ask you to think about the relationships between two things. The symbol : : means "is the same as" or "is analogous to."

Example: 5 : 25 : : 6 : ? would be read as "5 is to 25 as 6 is to what?"

The answer is 36 because 5 times itself is 25 and 6 times itself is 36.

Use the example above to answer these analogy puzzles.

a. 4 : 16 : : 10 : ?

Choose from: 12 32 25 100

b. Triangle : Hexagon : : Rectangle : ?

Choose from: Square Pentagon Line Octagon

16. By looking at the first three circles, can you see a pattern or relationship that is the same in all four circles? This pattern or relationship will help you determine the missing number in the last circle. What is that number?

HINT
Look to see how the numbers in each circle relate to each other.

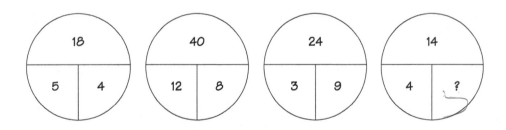

Copyright © 2009 by John Wiley & Sons, Inc.

17. Roman numerals are written as combinations of the seven letters below. They usually are written as capital letters because they are easier and less confusing to read.

Roman Numerals	
I = 1	C = 100
V = 5	D = 500
X = 10	M = 1,000
L = 50	

If smaller numbers follow larger numbers, the numbers are added. If a smaller number precedes a larger number, the smaller number is subtracted from the larger number. For example:

- VIII = 5 + 3 = 8

- IX = 10 − 1 = 9

- XL = 50 − 10 = 40

- XC = 100 − 10 = 90

- MCMLXXXIV = 1,000 + (1,000 − 100) + 50 + 30 + (5 − 1) = 1,984

Copyright © 2009 by John Wiley & Sons, Inc.

Roman Numeral Table							
1	I	14	XIV	27	XXVII	150	CL
2	II	15	XV	28	XXVIII	200	CC
3	III	16	XVI	29	XXIX	300	CCC
4	IV	17	XVII	30	XXX	400	CD
5	V	18	XVIII	31	XXXI	500	D
6	VI	19	XIX	40	XL	600	DC
7	VII	20	XX	50	L	700	DCC
8	VIII	21	XXI	60	LX	800	DCCC
9	IX	22	XXII	70	LXX	900	CM
10	X	23	XXIII	80	LXXX	1,000	M
11	XI	24	XXIV	90	XC	1,600	MDC
12	XII	25	XXV	100	C	1,700	MDCC
13	XIII	26	XXVI	101	CI	1,900	MCM

Change the following from Arabic to Roman and from Roman to Arabic numerals:

a. 59 = ?

b. 88 = ?

c. 449 = ?

d. MXLVII = ?

e. LXIX = ?

f. MCD = ?

g. 2,919 = ?

h. CMXCIX = ?

Copyright © 2009 by John Wiley & Sons, Inc.

18. Joan's sister scored 17 points in her school's basketball game. She had an even number of 2-point shots and an odd number of 3-point shots for her points. She attempted no freethrows. How many baskets of each type did Joan's sister make?

4-2   3-3

19. You can have lots of fun creating your own puzzles. Here's an example to get you started:

Write the numbers 1 through 9 in a straight line.

1   2   3   4   5   6   7   8   9

Now, depending upon what your goal is, you can insert the basic math operation symbols between the numbers and arrive at different totals.

$1 + 2 + 3 + 4 - 5 + 6 + 7 - 8 + 9 = 19$

$12 - 3 + 45 - 67 + 89 = 76$

$123 + 45 - 67 + 8 - 9 = 100$

Now try to get the answer 100 in different ways. Then try to create some problems of your own. (Don't forget—you can use multiplication and division, too.)

20. Which of the values below is the same as 7?

a. $(6 \times 5) \div 2$

b. $(3 + 4) \div 5$

c. $(10 - 4) + \dfrac{1}{1}$

d. $(12 - 5) + 2$

Copyright © 2009 by John Wiley & Sons, Inc.

21. Below is a pyramid of numbers where the number on each brick is the sum of two bricks below it. The numbers given will help you fill in the entire pyramid.

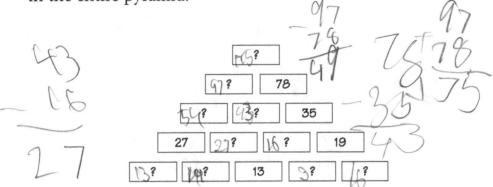

		175?		
	97?		78	
54?		43?		35
27	27?		16?		19
13?	14?		13		3?		16?

22. Use the clues to find these mystery numbers that include decimals.

"My hundredths number is one half my tenths number. My ones digit number is twice my tenths number. There is no number 1 in any of the three places."

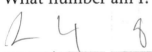

What number am I?

2 . 4   8

23. In the addition problem below, A, B, C, and D each stand for a different one-digit number.

None of the letters represents zero.

```
  A   +   7
 +B       6
 ──      ───
 DC      D5
```

If C is 5 and A is 7, then B is ? . 8

Copyright © 2009 by John Wiley & Sons, Inc.

24. The numbers 1 through 6 are placed in the triangle below so that each of the three sides totals 12. Using the same numbers, can they be placed around the triangle so that each side totals 9?

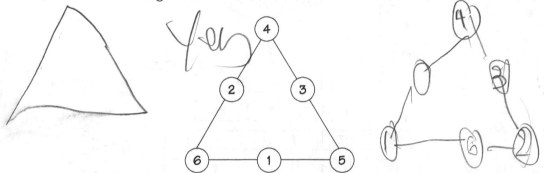

25. Solve the puzzle by putting back the parts that are missing. Equations are formed horizontally from left to right and vertically from top to bottom. Use both numbers and math operations (+, −, and = signs).

Copyright © 2009 by John Wiley & Sons, Inc.

Copyright © 2009 by John Wiley & Sons, Inc.

26. On one of my math travel excursions, I ended up in the far-off land of Footfree. The entire country of Footfree liked shoes, and all the residents had some of the neatest and strangest shoes I've ever seen. Everything they did had to do with shoes. Even their schools were built like army boots. All the problems in their math books used shoes as examples—like this problem.

Three fourth-graders had shoes sizes of 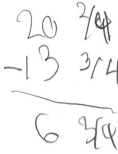 $6\frac{1}{3}$, $8\frac{1}{2}$, and $5\frac{2}{3}$ (yes, they had all kinds of fractional sizes).

Three fifth-graders had shoe sizes that added up to the same total as the sum of the fourth-graders' shoes.

Two of the fifth-graders' sizes were $7\frac{1}{4}$ and $6\frac{1}{2}$. What size was the third fifth-grader's shoe?

27. Also, in Footfree, the residents liked to combine adding and multiplication. They had a math operation called a "shoebox" that looked like this:

$$5 \boxed{} 3 \rightarrow 23$$

The shoebox between the 5 and the 3 meant that you had to add 5 + 3, then multiply 5 × 3, and then add those two sums together:

$$5 + 3 = 8$$
$$\underline{5 \times 3 = 15}$$
$$23$$

What does this shoebox puzzle equal?

$$4 \boxed{} 2 \quad + \quad 3 \boxed{} 6 \quad = \quad ?$$

28. Before I left Footfree, the kids in all the math classes had "Footfree Puzzle Day" and asked me to be their guest. It was great fun with lots of food. Here is the puzzle they gave me to remember my time in their wonderful school:

Tennis shoes → $4.00 (Footfree dollars)

Snow boots → $3.00

Slippers → $2.00

Flip-flops → $2.00

All of the above prices are based on a simple math concept. Based on these prices, what would a pair of loafers cost?

a. $1.00

b. $3.00

c. $4.00

d. $8.00

Copyright © 2009 by John Wiley & Sons, Inc.

29. Here's a fun puzzle game called Circle Squeeze. Each circle has two numbers. For each pair of circles, the sum of their two numbers is the same, like this:

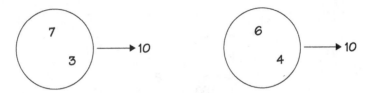

But the circles are like magnets. They crash into each other, and one number from each circle is added to one number from the other circle.

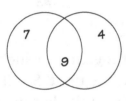

You can see here that the 3 from the circle on the left has been added to the 6 from the second circle to form the sum of 9. Now here's the puzzle:

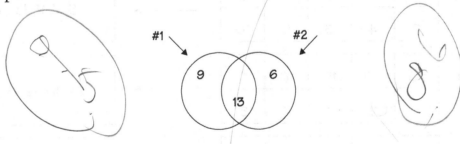

What are the two numbers that go back into circle #1 and circle #2? In other words, what did these two circles look like before they were "squeezed" into each other? Is there an easy way to solve this?

Copyright © 2009 by John Wiley & Sons, Inc.

30. What if there are three circles? What did these three circles look like before they were squeezed into each other?

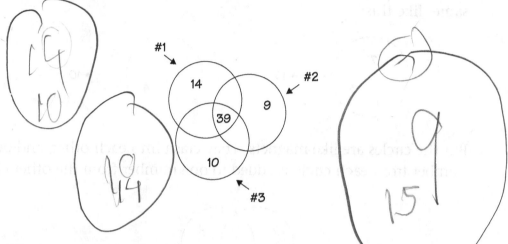

31. The boxes on the left fit together in such a way that their numbers help to build the box on the right. See if you can determine how the numbers in the two rows on the left make the numbers on the right, then fill in the missing numbers.

a.

1	3	5	7	9
2	4	6	8	10

→ 3, 7, 11, 15, _?_ 19

b.

25	20	15	10	5
1	2	3	4	5

→ 24, 18, 12, 6, _?_ 0

c.

4	5	10	12	7
12	20	30	36	49

→ 3, 4, 3, 3, _?_ 7

d.

50	40	30	20	10
2	4	6	8	10

→ 100, 160, 180, 160, _?_ 100

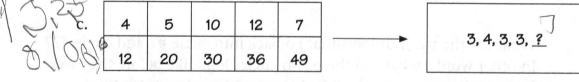

32. My friend Billy needs some help. His math teacher told him to take a look at the addition problem below.

$$\begin{array}{r} 16 \\ +69 \\ \hline 85 \end{array}$$

The teacher then asked him what are the fewest number of single digits that would have to be changed for the sum to be 160 instead of 85. Can you help Billy? Here are the choices:

a. 1 digit—the 1

b. 2 digits—the 1 and the 6 in "69"

c. 3 digits—the 9 and the 1 and 6 in "16"

d. 2 digits—the 1 and the 9

33. The numbers in the corners of the boxes below fit together in such a way that they determine the number in the middle of each box. The rule for finding that middle number is the same in each box.

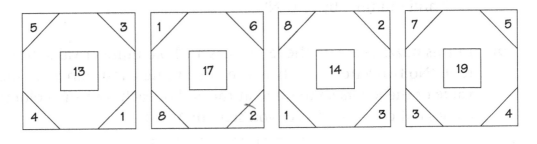

Once you find that rule, see if you can put the correct number in this box:

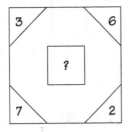

Copyright © 2009 by John Wiley & Sons, Inc.

34. What number or numbers comes next in this series?

| 1 | 22 | 333 | 4444 | 55555 | 666666 | ? |

35. Here's a fun puzzle game called FTN (Find This Number). It works like this:

I'll give you some instruction, and you put the clues together and write down the answer. Here's an example:

7 < this number < 12. This number is often used when speaking about cats. FTN!

Answer: The number is 9. Because 9 is more than 7 and less than 12, and cats are said to have 9 lives. Now try these:

a. 3 < this number < 7. This number is between two other numbers that total 10. FTN!

b. 15 > this number > 9 and exactly in the middle of the two numbers mentioned here. FTN!

c. This number is (5 × 2) + 3 + 7 – 6. Take that result and divide by 7 and multiply by 3. FTN!

36. In this puzzle, each of the letters has a whole-number value from 1 to 9. (No two letters can share the same value.) Your job is to find the value of the letters so the sum at the end of each row and column comes out correctly. To get you started: A = 3.

D	E	B	E	E	28
E	C	D	E	E	31
A	E	A	B	D	22
C	B	A	E	B	15
C	A	D	E	C	26
26	20	25	25	26	

Copyright © 2009 by John Wiley & Sons, Inc.

Copyright © 2009 by John Wiley & Sons, Inc.

37. In this arithmetic puzzle you have to fill in the question marks in the equations with numbers or one of the three operation symbols: +, −, ×. (This puzzle has no division.)

4	×	3	−	9	+	8	11
+	■	+	■	+	■	+	
8	×	9	+	3	−	?	71
+	■	×	■	+	■	−	
9	×	4	+	4	?	1	41
×	■	?	■	×	■	+	
3	+	8	−	?	?	9	18

39 31 20 20

38. Can you place the numbers 1, 4, 5, 6, 7, and 0 in the boxes below? Each number can be used once and only once. There is more than one correct answer.

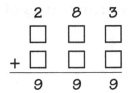

$$\begin{array}{cccc} & 2 & 8 & 3 \\ & \square & \square & \square \\ + & \square & \square & \square \\ \hline & 9 & 9 & 9 \end{array}$$

39. The numbers 1–9 can be placed in the nine circles below in such a way that both sets of crossed circles can add up to 26. From the numbers already given, where would the number 1 go? It can be placed in either one of two circles.

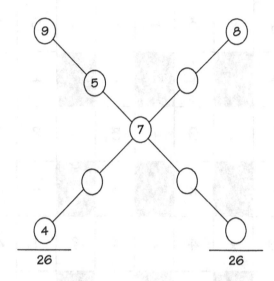

40. In a group of 28 junior high school students, 7 take French, 10 take Spanish, and 4 take both languages. The students taking both French and Spanish are not counted with the 7 taking French or the 10 taking Spanish. How many students are not taking either French or Spanish?

41. A fruit dealer packages pears in two different box sizes. One size holds 5 pears and the other size holds 12 pears. The dealer sold 68 pears in one of the stores in one hour. He said to his assistant, "You don't see that very often. We sold the same number of boxes of each type of packaging." How many boxes of each size did they sell in one hour?

Copyright © 2009 by John Wiley & Sons, Inc.

Just for Fun: Frame Game

42. Find the hidden phrase or title.

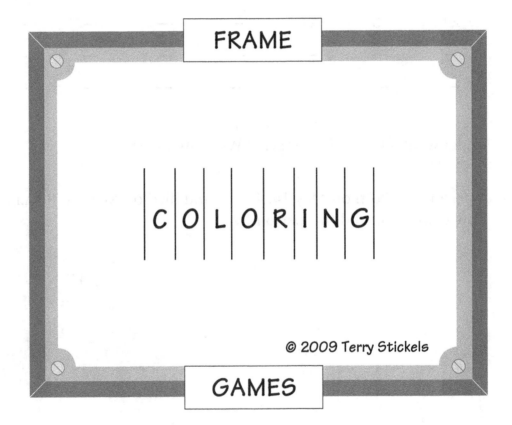

FRAME

COLORING

© 2009 Terry Stickels

GAMES

43. Suppose all numbers from 1 to 1,000 are arranged in columns like they are below.

A	B	C	D	E	F	G
1	2	3	4	5	6	7
8	9	10	11	12	13	14
15	16	17	18	19	20	21
22	23	24	—	—	—	—
—	—	—	—	—	—	—
—	—	—	—	—	—	—

Under what letter will 50 appear? What about 100?

44. A person was born on May 14, 40 B.C. and died on May 14, 30 A.D. How many years did this person live?

HINT
Try using a number line.

Copyright © 2009 by John Wiley & Sons, Inc.

45. Below is a fun type of puzzle called a Number Scramble or an Equation Scramble. The numbers and operations are scrambled, so you'll have to move things around so the equation will make sense. You must use all the parts in the boxes on the left-hand side of the equation to arrive at the solution on the right-hand side of the equation.

Here is an example:

| 3 | | 5 | | × | | 7 | | + | | ( ) | | = | | 56 |

One solution is:

$$(3 + 5) \times 7 = 56$$

Now try these:

a. | 6 | | 4 | | ( ) | | + | | 2 | | × | | = | | 32 |

b. | × | | 4 | | + | | 5 | | ( ) | | 5 | | 1 | | + | | = | | 50 | | ( ) |

c. | × | | ÷ | | 2 | | ( ) | | 3 | | × | | 4 | | 6 | | = | | 4 |

d. | 1 | | + | | + | | 2 | | 3 | | ÷ | | 6 | | = | | ( ) | | 1 |

46. Complete the table using the pattern already created by the numbers you see. Fill in the last three boxes.

10	7	8
13	11	9
16	15	11
19	19	14
22	23	18
?	?	?

Copyright © 2009 by John Wiley & Sons, Inc.

47. A certain whole number is evenly divisible by 3. It is also divisible by 5 and 4. What is the smallest number that fits these conditions? Can you find a number larger than 100 that is divisible by 3, 4, and 5?

48. One of the following numbers does not belong with the others in each of the three puzzles. The other numbers have a similarity the "odd one out" does not have. Which one does not belong?

a.

	7		63		56
		21		28		36

b.

	63		18		72
54		45		36		26

c.

	16		64		45
24		48		8	

49. Using the 3 × 3 grid below, answer the following questions:

25	13	37
42	8	9
66	58	34

a. The number beneath the number that is to the left of the number that is 37 is ? .

b. The sum of three of the numbers in the squares equals 100. Two of the numbers multiplied together equals 225. What are the three numbers?

c. The sum of the numbers in the two diagonals is 20 more than the sum of this row or column. Which row or column is it?

Copyright © 2009 by John Wiley & Sons, Inc.

50. Two friends were playing a ring toss game where you throw 10 rings over the tops of cylinders 15 feet away. For each ring that goes over a cylinder, you receive 5 points. For each ring that misses, you lose 3 points. One of the friends scored 26 and the other scored 18. How many rings did each have that were successful tosses?

51. Look carefully at the numbers in each row of the pyramid below. See if you can find a relationship or pattern to determine the number that goes at the top of the pyramid.

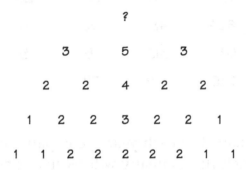

```
                        ?

                 3      5      3

             2     2    4    2    2

          1    2   2   3   2   2   1

        1   1   2   2   2   2   2   1   1
```

52. In the equations below, replace each asterisk with one of the four math operations signs: +, −, ×, ÷. Each sign can be used once and only once. The parentheses have been placed for you.

HINT
The first sign is +.

a. (8 * 7) * 6 * (6 * 1) = 18

b. 5 * 4 * 3 * 2 * 1 = 7

Copyright © 2009 by John Wiley & Sons, Inc.

53. The second, third, and fourth numbers in each row below are determined by a simple method applied to the first number in each row. The procedure is the same for each row. See if you can determine how the second, third, and fourth numbers in each row were determined, and fill in the missing blank.

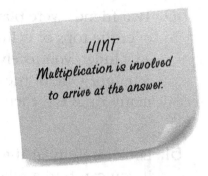

HINT
Multiplication is involved to arrive at the answer.

384	96	54	20
624	48	32	6
579	315	15	5
739	189	72	___

54. Starting on January 1 of each year, a company has set up a delivery schedule in which the company will receive paper supplies every 2 days, bottled water every 3 days, and electrical supplies every 4 days. How often do the paper supplies, water, and electrical supplies arrive on the same day? On how many total days throughout the year will all three arrive?

Copyright © 2009 by John Wiley & Sons, Inc.

55. Here are some more arithmetic square puzzles. Find the missing numbers or operation symbols that complete the equations.

a.

9	−	1	−	?	= 2
+	■	×	■	+	
?	×	7	×	4	= 56
×	■	×	■	×	
5	×	8	+	?	= 43
=		=		=	
19		56		18	

b.

7	+	9	−	?	= 12
+	■	+	■	−	
2	+	6	−	?	= 7
×	■	×	■	+	
8	+	3	+	5	= 16
=		=		=	
23		27		8	

c.

?	×	8	×	3	= 24
×	■	−	■	×	
?	−	?	+	6	= 13
×	■	×	■	×	
7	×	5	+	?	= 39
=		=		=	
63		2		72	

d.

1	×	?	×	2	= 16
×	■	−	■	×	
?	×	6	+	?	= 37
+	■	×	■	−	
3	×	9	×	4	= 108
=		=		=	
8		46		10	

Copyright © 2009 by John Wiley & Sons, Inc.

56. This is a fun puzzle called Addiply. It combines both addition and multiplication.

Using the numbers 1 through 9 (you can use higher numbers as you become more proficient at solving these), look for combinations of two numbers to find the ones whose sum and product match the numbers given. Here's an example:

1st Number	2nd Number	Sum	Product
3	4	7	12
4	6	10	24
?	?	6	8

Answer: The two missing numbers are 2 and 4 (in either order).

Now try these:

	1st Number	2nd Number	Sum	Product
a.	5	?	14	45
b.	?	?	8	15
c.	?	?	13	36
d.	?	?	9	8

Copyright © 2009 by John Wiley & Sons, Inc.

Just for Fun: Frame Game

57. Find the hidden phrase or title.

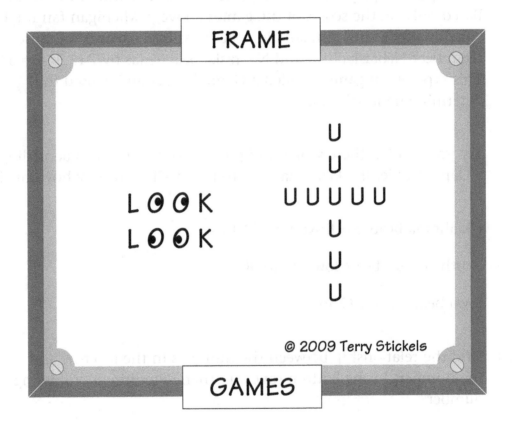

FRAME

L👁👁K
L👁👁K

U
U
UUUUU
U
U
U

© 2009 Terry Stickels

GAMES

58. Below are some football scores from a fictitious college football season. One of the things fans like to do is compare scores of different games to see what might happen if two of their favorite teams might meet in a game later in the year—maybe in a Bowl game.

For example, let's say Michigan beat Nebraska 24 to 20. Later that season Nebraska beat Texas 17 to 10. Then it is decided that Michigan will play Texas in the Rose Bowl at the end of the season. Based only on the scores of the games above, a Michigan fan might conclude that Michigan should beat Texas by 11 points, because the team beat Nebraska by 4 and Nebraska beat Texas by 7 (7 + 4 = 11). This type of fan game is called a Game Ladder and is used to determine national rankings.

Try your skill at these scores and predict who would win according to a Game Ladder if Oklahoma were to play UCLA. And by how much?

Oklahoma beats Northwestern 21 to 7

Northwestern beats Iowa 31 to 30

Iowa beats UCLA 17 to 10

59. Find the relationship between the numbers in the top row and the numbers in the bottom row, and then determine the missing number.

12	24	36	45	60	84
6	8	9	9	10	?

Copyright © 2009 by John Wiley & Sons, Inc.

60. Below is a "subtraction triangle," where the numbers directly below the two numbers above them result from subtracting the two numbers. The numbers in the following example are from 1 to 15, and each number is only used once.

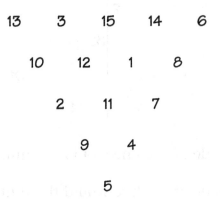

Notice that $13 - 3 = 10$, $15 - 3 = 12$, $8 - 1 = 7$, $9 - 4 = 5$, etc. As you can see from the $15 - 3$ example, the two numbers can be subtracted in any order.

Now see if you can build a subtraction triangle using the numbers 1 to 10. I'll help get you started by supplying a few numbers.

Copyright © 2009 by John Wiley & Sons, Inc.

61. The numbers on each side of the line are grouped together for a specific reason because they share a basic feature in common.

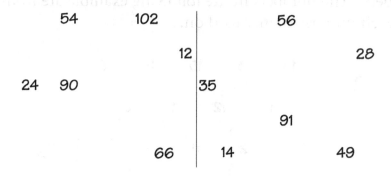

a. On what side of the line would the number 98 fit?

b. On what side of the line would the number 18 fit?

c. What is a number that might fit on either side?

62. Bess weighs 20 pounds less than her brother Brandon. Together they weigh 120 pounds. What does each weigh?

63. Here's an alphametic puzzle where each letter stands for a positive whole number between 0 and 9. Zero (0) cannot begin a word. I'll help you get started.

$$
\begin{array}{r}
ICE \\
+CREAM \\
\hline
CAKES
\end{array}
$$

Let A = 3
I = 9
R = 2
S = 8

Copyright © 2009 by John Wiley & Sons, Inc.

64. Here's another alphametic puzzle. Each letter has a digit value. Zero (0) cannot begin a word. I'll give you some hints to get you started. When completed properly, this will be a correct addition problem.

$$
\begin{array}{r}
\text{THIS} \\
+\ \text{IS} \\
\hline
\text{NEAT}
\end{array}
$$

Let A = 7
T = 2
The number 1 is not in this puzzle.

65. In Nina's class the ratio of boys to girls is 5 to 3. There are 10 more boys than girls. How many girls and boys are there in Nina's class?

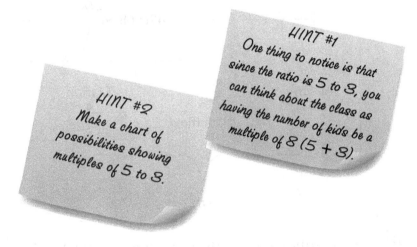

HINT #1
One thing to notice is that since the ratio is 5 to 3, you can think about the class as having the number of kids be a multiple of 8 (5 + 3).

HINT #2
Make a chart of possibilities showing multiples of 5 to 3.

Copyright © 2009 by John Wiley & Sons, Inc.

66. Jim and his mom were taking a vacation from their home in Albion to a lake resort in Deer Park. The total distance from Albion to Deer Park is 470 miles. Jim knows that the distance from Albion to Clarion is 270 miles. Jim's mom also had told him that the distance from Bloomfield to Deer Park is 350 miles. But neither Jim nor his mom was sure of the distance from Bloomfield to Clarion. Note that Bloomfield and Clarion are between Albion and Deer Park (see the diagram below). Can you help Jim and his mom find the distance from Bloomfield to Clarion with the information given?

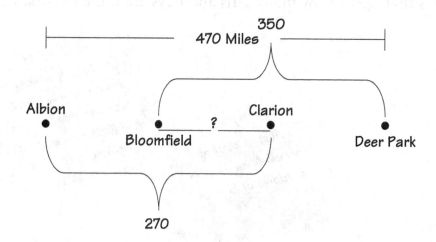

67. In the following words, the letters in the alphabet each have been given a number, following a logical sequence. If C = 3, E = 5, S = 19, I = 9, A + T = 21, and C + A + T = 24, can you figure out what number these words equal?

B + E + E = ?   G + A + M + E = ?

Z + O + O = ?   S + C + H + O + O + L = ?

D + O + G = ?   I + S + L + A + N + D = ?

68. Carla was enjoying her new calculator and discovering all the features and functions. She accidentally multiplied a number by 5 when she should have divided by 5. The incorrect answer displayed was 75. What should have been the correct answer?

a. 3   c. 15

b. 6   d. 25

Copyright © 2009 by John Wiley & Sons, Inc.

Copyright © 2009 by John Wiley & Sons, Inc.

69. Here's a puzzle called Triple Diamonduzzle. The numbers in the two sets of diamond figures on top have a relationship that determines the number inside the small diamond on the bottom. Here's an example:

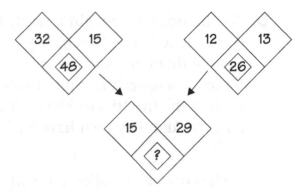

Answer: 45

The numbers on top are added together. The number found in the smaller diamond on the bottom is one more than the sum of those two numbers.

$$32 + 15 = 47 \qquad 12 + 13 = 25 \qquad 15 + 29 = 44$$

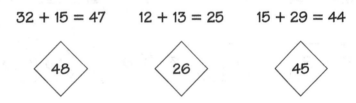

Try these Triple Diamonduzzles:

a.

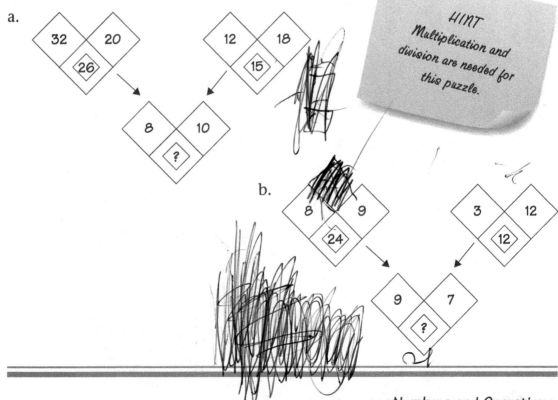

HINT
Multiplication and division are needed for this puzzle.

b.

70. Five friends each bought a candy bar and a drink at the local convenience store. When they checked to see how much money each of them had left, the answer was surprising. Each had less than 50 cents, and each had just 4 coins. No one had pennies or quarters. Each of the five friends had a different amount of money. What amounts did they each have left?

71. Each series below follows its own logical rules. Can you determine the next number in each series?

a.

b.
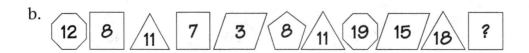

c. 7 → 9 → 11 ⇉ 15 → 17 ⇉ 21 ⇉ ?

Copyright © 2009 by John Wiley & Sons, Inc.

Just for Fun: Frame Game

72. Find the hidden phrase or title.

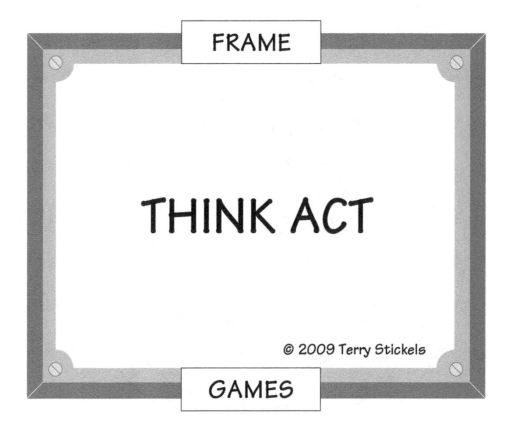

FRAME

THINK ACT

© 2009 Terry Stickels

GAMES

73. Elise took an archery class last summer. The targets had an unusual scoring system, shown in the illustration below. One of the weekly goals was to shoot arrows into the targets where the total would be exactly 100. For example, two arrows, one of which landed inside 72, the other of which landed in 28, would total 100. Another example might be seven arrows that landed like this: 3, 9, 12, 15, 18, 28, and 15 again. Can you come up with two more sets of numbers? What number must always be in any group to reach 100? Why does that number have to be in any grouping?

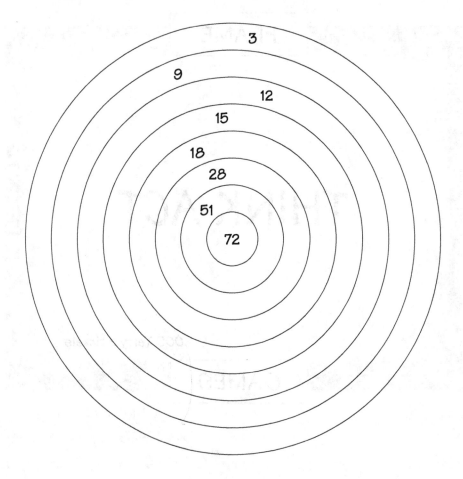

Copyright © 2009 by John Wiley & Sons, Inc.

74. This is a very old puzzle that goes like this:

As I was going to Saint Ives,

I crossed the path of seven wives.

Every wife had seven sacks,

Every sack had seven cats,

Every cat had seven kittens,

Kittens, cats, sacks, wives,

How many were going to Saint Ives?

Two answers usually are given. The first answer is one. Since the narrator was going to Saint Ives, the seven wives must have been leaving Saint Ives because the narrator crossed their paths. The other answer is the one many people come up with: 2,801 (7 wives, 49 sacks, 343 cats, and 2,401 kittens equal 2,800. Then you have to add one more for the person speaking the words of the riddle.)

Now, here's our version. How many of each are there?

Five by five they walked my way

Side by side their arms did sway.

Gold pips on their shoulders

To carry the day.

Brass-tipped swords

Full battle array.

Each with white gloves

They were a sight to see

Each glove with a star

Silver and shiny.

And the stars had five points

Just like you thought

Would cost you a fortune

For you to have bought.

So, soldiers and pips

And swords with brass tips

White gloves with a star

Five points seen afar.

Add them together

Would you kind sir?

Tell me the total

My mind is a blur.

Copyright © 2009 by John Wiley & Sons, Inc.

75. Find the pattern starting with the first four numbers and moving to the right, and then fill in the missing number.

3	15		7	4		2	45		10	66		12	?
5	6		1	21		9	8		11	50		20	72

Now, using any whole numbers you wish, create your own grid of four numbers that will continue the sequence above.

76. The grid below has a specific pattern that determines the numbers in each box. What are the missing four numbers?

9	6	2	1
15	12	8	7
21	18	14	?
27	24	20	19
?	30	?	?

77. Here is a number cross where the sum in both directions is 23 (using the numbers 1–9 once and only once).

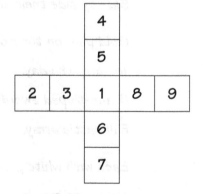

Now create a number cross that has a cross sum of 24 using the numbers 1–9 once and only once. (There are several possible variations, but the number in the middle will always be the same.)

Copyright © 2009 by John Wiley & Sons, Inc.

Copyright © 2009 by John Wiley & Sons, Inc.

78. All but one of these numbers share a
common factor. Which number is the odd
one out? What is the common factor?

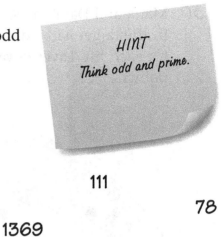

HINT
Think odd and prime.

185   407   111

37   78

740   1369

79. Can you fill in each of the boxes so the number in a rectangle is the
product of the two numbers beneath it?

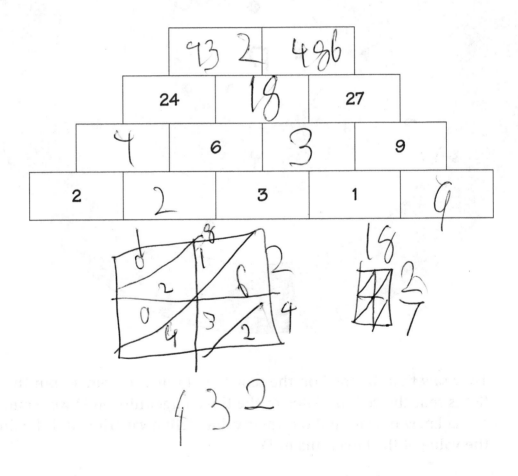

80. Maria and Damian were playing a bull's-eye game where each layer in the target had a different point value. Layer A was worth 1 point for each hit. Layer B was worth 5 points for each, and Layer C was 10 points.

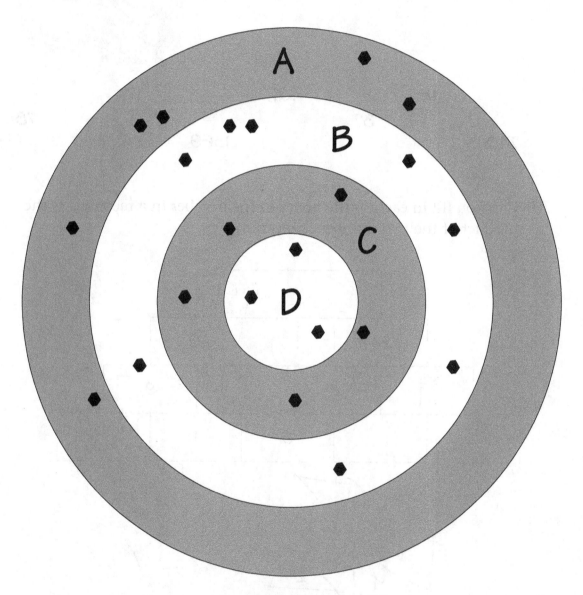

They saw that the total on the scoreboard was 156 points—but the lights that showed the value of the three target hits on D were out. Maria knew how to find out their value right away. How did she find the value of the target hits in D?

Copyright © 2009 by John Wiley & Sons, Inc.

Copyright © 2009 by John Wiley & Sons, Inc.

81. The numbers in Circle A below are factors of 6. The numbers in Circle B are factors of 8.

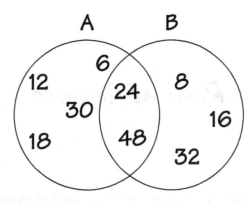

Where do the following numbers go?

a. 72

b. 40

c. 36

d. 25

e. 480

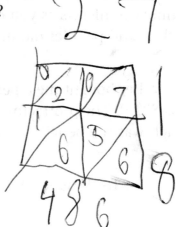

82. The numbers in Circle A below are factors of 7. The numbers in Circle B are factors of 3. Pick three numbers that will fit in the shaded area.

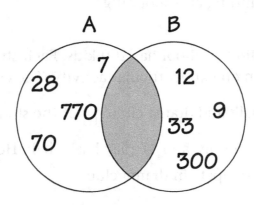

Rational Numbers

83. My sister gave me a bunch of pennies and nickels in change for a dollar bill and two dimes. She then said to me, "You have the same number of nickels as you do pennies in that $1.20." How many nickels and pennies did my sister give me?

84. My father bought me a pencil and a protractor. Together, the cost was $3.00. The protractor was $2.00 more than the pencil. How much was the pencil?

85. 9 is $\frac{1}{2}$ of 18; 18 is $\frac{1}{2}$ of 36. What is 72 divided by $\frac{1}{2}$?

86. Brady goes running for $\frac{3}{4}$ of an hour. When he comes home, he goes shopping with his mom for $\frac{2}{3}$ of an hour. How many minutes does Brady spend running and shopping?

87. Central Park Middle School has 100 kids. Each student is required to participate in an extracurricular activity. The choices are band, tennis, basketball, and drama club. $\frac{3}{10}$ of the students are in band, $\frac{1}{10}$ are in tennis, and 17 play basketball. How many students are going to participate in drama club?

Copyright © 2009 by John Wiley & Sons, Inc.

88. Try to match the left column with the appropriate number in the right column. You may not know each one, but you might be able to make some "educated guesses" that can get you the correct answer.

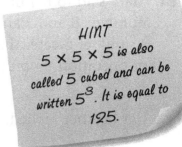

HINT
5 × 5 × 5 is also called 5 cubed and can be written 5^3. It is equal to 125.

a. 4^3 14

b. $\dfrac{1}{8} + \dfrac{1}{8}$ $\dfrac{1}{4}$

c. $\dfrac{5}{9}$ 64

d.   XIV   .555 . . .

89. See if you can place these fractions from lowest to highest value. I'll get you started. $\dfrac{1}{10}$ has the least value.

$$\frac{3}{5} \qquad \frac{1}{10} \qquad \frac{15}{17} \qquad \frac{1}{5} \qquad \frac{4}{9} \qquad \frac{1}{3}$$

90. Below is a box divided into different-sized squares with musical notes in each grid. What fraction of the entire big box would be represented by the small box with the question mark?

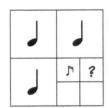

HINT
If you know music, then you know ♩ is a quarter note.

Copyright © 2009 by John Wiley & Sons, Inc.

91. Mary said to her brother, "I was given an assignment to use the numbers 8 and 9 and any math symbol or operation I want, to make a number greater than 8 but less than 9. I can use only one symbol or operation. I don't think it can be done."

Her brother replied, "I can do it in five seconds. Period."

If the word "period" is a hint, how did her brother do it?

92. Rolando is making a cake and needs exactly 6 cups of milk for the recipe. He has small containers of milk that he can use, but they come in only $\frac{3}{4}$-cup containers.

> *HINT*
> *There are several ways to think about this. What if he needed 3 cups of milk for the recipe instead?*

How many smaller containers would be needed to have the 6 cups he needs for the recipe?

93. Our baseball team won the league championship. For our awards dinner, the team had a pizza party. Each giant pizza was cut into 12 pieces. When they brought the giant pepperoni pizza, Jimmy grabbed $\frac{1}{3}$ of the entire pizza, Mark took $\frac{1}{6}$ of the pizza, Ernie grabbed $\frac{1}{4}$, and Roberto took $\frac{1}{6}$. How many individual pieces were left of the giant pepperoni pizza?

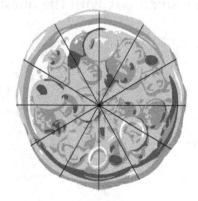

Copyright © 2009 by John Wiley & Sons, Inc.

94. Here's a fun puzzle. See how many different ways you can put three 3's together. You can use any math symbols you wish. For example:

$$(3 \times 3) + 3 = 12 \quad or \quad 3 \times \frac{3}{3} = 3 \quad or \quad \frac{(3 \div 3)}{3} = \frac{1}{3}$$

a. Can you make three 3's equal 11?

b. How about using three 3's to make 4?

c. Try making three 3's equal $\frac{1}{2}$.

95.

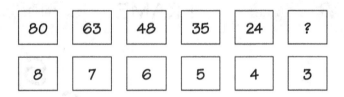

What is the relationship between the top and bottom boxes of each set, and which of the following might fit in the box with the question mark?

a. 20

b. 18

c. 47

d. 15

Copyright © 2009 by John Wiley & Sons, Inc.

Just for Fun: Frame Game

96. Find the hidden phrase or title.

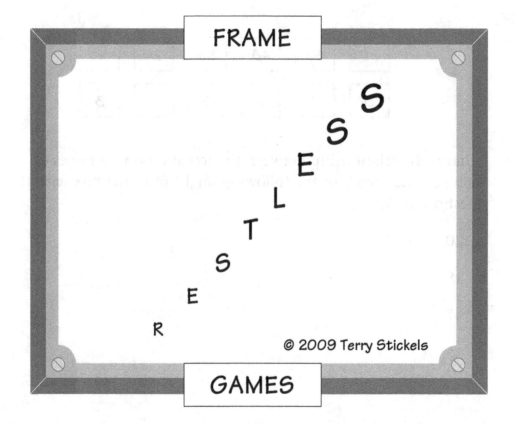

FRAME

RESTLESS

© 2009 Terry Stickels

GAMES

97. Marty's father has work crews who cut trees. He has one crew of six men who can cut 10 trees in a day. He is going to send them on a project where they need to cut 30 trees. How many days will it take this crew to accomplish this?

3

On the next project after this, Marty's dad has decided to increase the crew to 12 men. This new project has 20 trees. So, with 20 trees and 12 men, how long will the crew take to complete the work?

1 day

98. What is the value of the following expression?

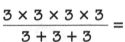

$$\frac{3 \times 3 \times 3 \times 3}{3 + 3 + 3} =$$

a. 5

b. 3

c. 9

99. Which of the following fractions are less than $\frac{1}{3}$?

a. $\frac{15}{46}$ b. $\frac{33}{90}$ c. $\frac{5}{12}$ d. $\frac{101}{300}$

100. Amelia's father works in a chocolate factory that makes 400 pounds of chocolate into a big brick, then shaves off enough to package it into boxes that hold 2.5 pounds of chocolate each. Each box then is sold for $10. What is the total selling price of all 400 pounds of chocolate?

1330

101. Allison has $.82 in coins. There are no more than two of any one coin. (There is not a $.50 piece.) Can you tell me how many coins Allison has?

Copyright © 2009 by John Wiley & Sons, Inc.

102. Matt made the circle graph below to show how many students in his school had pets. Of the total students, 180 students gave Matt the information and 20 said they had no pets.

a. What fraction of the students had a dog?

b. How many students is that?

c. What is the fraction of bird owners compared to dog owners?

d. How many students are represented by kids who own fish, cats, and no pets?

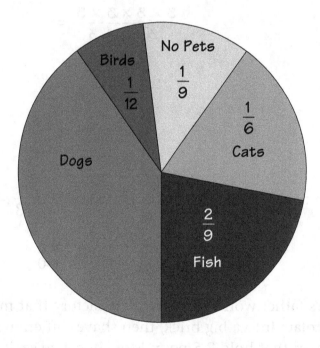

Copyright © 2009 by John Wiley & Sons, Inc.

103.

Here is a puzzle made just for you:
The clues are right there, but just a few.

Pennies and nickels in my pocket for now
Add in some quarters and I'll tell you how

To add up the total with some dimes there, too.

Five of the first—now that's just a start
Eight of the dimes—but that's only part.

Quarter and nickels—the number's the same.
Are you still with me now, your head in the game?

Twenty-one total, that is the count.
Coins in my pocket, no small amount.

So tell me, my friends, what do you see?
How much money for you and for me?

104. Olivia needed change for the bus. She exchanged a $1 bill and two quarters for nickels and dimes. When she looked at what she had been given, she was surprised to see the same number of nickels and dimes. How many of each did she have?

105. Janie's dad asked her this question at dinner, and she wasn't sure of the answer. Could you help her?

"You have three numbers, and two of those numbers are $\frac{2}{3}$ and $\frac{3}{4}$. What should the third number be so all three numbers average 2?

Copyright © 2009 by John Wiley & Sons, Inc.

106. Amara was reading a book about a funny monster who had a paisley toenail. When Prozillio (the name of the monster) tried to cut his toenail, 2 more grew back. When he cut these two, 4 toenails grew back. Of course, he couldn't believe his eyes, so he cut the 4 toenails and 8 grew back. So, after 3 cuttings, he had 8 toenails. What if Prozillio kept cutting? How many toenails would he have after 7 cuts?

107. What number goes where the question mark is?

$$\frac{1}{2}+\frac{1}{4}+\frac{1}{8}+\frac{1}{16}=\frac{15}{16}$$

$$\frac{1}{4}+\frac{1}{8}+\frac{1}{16}+\frac{1}{32}=\frac{15}{32}$$

$$\frac{1}{8}+\frac{1}{16}+\frac{1}{32}+\frac{1}{64}=\frac{?}{64}$$

108. Here's a fun fraction sequence. Can you find the missing number?

$$\frac{1}{2}\quad\frac{1}{6}\quad\frac{1}{3}\quad\frac{1}{5}\quad\frac{1}{4}\quad\frac{1}{4}\quad\frac{1}{5}\quad\frac{1}{3}\quad\frac{1}{6}\quad ?$$

HINT
Instead of looking at each fraction in order from left to right, try skipping around!

109. If I have 1 penny, 1 nickel, 1 dime, and 1 quarter, what fraction of $1.00 do I have?

Copyright © 2009 by John Wiley & Sons, Inc.

110. Below are two number lines. One is marked for every third number. The other is marked for every fifth number. If you placed one number line on top of the other, the origins would be the same. The numbers 3 and 5 would be together, 6 and 10 would be together, etc. The same for the negative numbers: (−3, −5) (−6, −10).

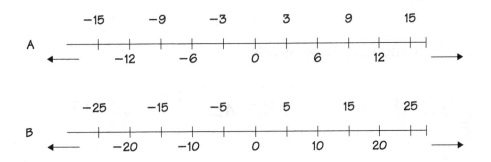

a. When line B reaches 100, what number will be read at the end of line A that is on top of line B?

b. If a point on line A reads −24, what is the same point on line B?

Copyright © 2009 by John Wiley & Sons, Inc.

Just for Fun: Frame Game

111. Find the hidden phrase or title.

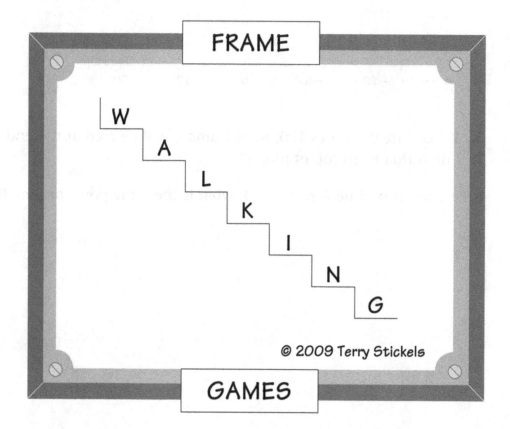

FRAME

W
  A
    L
      K
        I
          N
            G

© 2009 Terry Stickels

GAMES

112. You can use four 9's to make 99: $(9 \times 9) + (9 + 9) = 81 + 18 = 99$

You can use four 9's to make 2: $\dfrac{9}{9} + \dfrac{9}{9} = 1 + 1 = 2$

You can use four 9's to make 990:
$$\begin{array}{r} 999 \\ -\ 9 \\ \hline 990 \end{array}$$

But can you make four 9's equal 100?

113. The fractions and percentages in the left-hand column have equivalent values in the right-hand column. Can you match them?

Examples: $\dfrac{5}{8} = .625$

$$37\% = \dfrac{37}{100}$$

$$\dfrac{1}{2} \div 5 = \dfrac{1}{10}$$

a. $\dfrac{2}{5} \times \dfrac{5}{8}$ $\dfrac{11}{25}$

b. $\dfrac{3}{8}$ $\dfrac{5}{6}$

c. 44% $\dfrac{1}{4}$

d. $\dfrac{2}{9}$ .2222…

e. $\dfrac{1}{3} + \dfrac{1}{2}$ .375

f. 4.4%   .044

Copyright © 2009 by John Wiley & Sons, Inc.

114. A pan of brownies 9″ × 9″ serves 8 people. How many people will a pan of 18″ × 18″ serve?

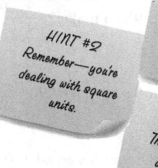

HINT #1
Be careful! Take a close look at what is needed.

HINT #2
Remember—you're dealing with square units.

HINT #3
Think of comparing area to people.

115. Zara's dad said he had just driven the 3 miles home from work in 4 minutes, without stopping. How many miles per hour is 3 miles in 4 minutes?

116. Which of these are bigger?

a. (1) 171 hundredths × 171 hundredths

(2) 1.71000 × 1.71000

(3) They are the same.

b. (1) $\frac{1}{2}+\frac{1}{7}$

(2) $\frac{1}{3}+\frac{1}{6}$

(3) $\frac{1}{4}+\frac{1}{5}$

(4) They are the same.

Copyright © 2009 by John Wiley & Sons, Inc.

117. There are 60 seconds in 1 minute. There are 60 minutes in 1 hour. There are 5,280 ft. in 1 mile. So what are the following in miles per hour?

a. 88 ft./sec. = ? miles/hr.

b. 440 ft./sec. = ? miles/hr.

118. The school's copying machine needs repairs. It will not make copies that are the exact size of the document being copied. In other words, there is no 100% button. Copies can be made larger and smaller. For example, the 200% button works, so copies can be made twice as large. The 50% button works, so copies can be made $\frac{1}{2}$ their original size. The machine also has 40% and 20% buttons. Pam knows that she can make a 100% copy by blowing up the original to 200% and then pushing the 50% button, so she feels comfortable making copies of different sizes by pushing the buttons in different combinations.

a. How can she make a document $\frac{1}{4}$ its original size (25%)?

b. 80% its original size?

c. What happens if she mistakenly pushes the 20% three times? What percentage or fraction will the size of the document be?

119. Laura saw that there were three pieces of candy left in a bowl on the kitchen table. She knew they were either chocolates or caramels but didn't know how many of each. What is the probability that there is a piece of chocolate candy in the bowl?

a. $\frac{1}{2}$

b. $\frac{7}{8}$

c. $\frac{1}{3}$

d. Can't tell

Copyright © 2009 by John Wiley & Sons, Inc.

120. In the diagram below, the circles above the crossbar have a value of 1. These below the bar have a value of 5. The bold black line is 0 (zero). The numbers to the left are whole numbers (ones, tens, hundreds, thousands). The numbers to the right of the bold line are fractions (tenths, hundredths, and thousandths).

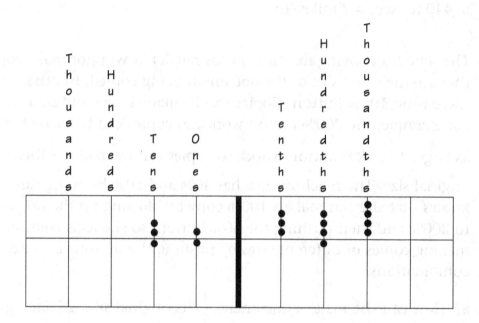

What number do the circles represent?

a. 120.371

b. 36.281

c. 76.344

d. 76.384

Copyright © 2009 by John Wiley & Sons, Inc.

121. A grocery store recently did a survey of its customers to see what kinds of candy they preferred. Of the 1,000 people surveyed, 48% liked *Chocolate Crunchers*. Of that 48%, one-third thought it was the second best-tasting candy bar, and of that group, 25% thought it was the third best-tasting candy bar. All the rest who weren't in the above percentages thought it was the best-tasting candy.

How many thought it was the third best-tasting candy bar? How many thought it was the best-tasting candy?

122. What is $\dfrac{1}{2}$ of $\dfrac{1}{3}$ of $36 \times 6 \div \dfrac{1}{2}$?

123. What is 37% of 37% of 37% of 37% of 1?

    a. .1369 squared

    b. .37 to the 4th power

    c. 1.87%

    d. All of the above

Copyright © 2009 by John Wiley & Sons, Inc.

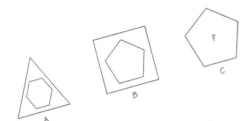

Part II

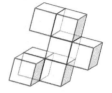

GEOMETRY
and
MEASUREMENT

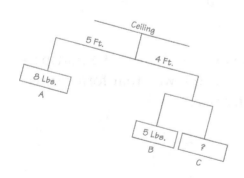

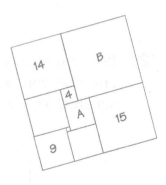

Geometry

124. There are 11 ways to unfold a cube into a flat, two-dimensional shape. A two-dimensional pattern that can be folded into a three-dimensional shape is called a net. One of the nets below cannot be folded into a cube. Which one is it?

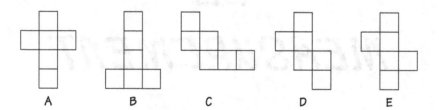

125. Below are two squares of the same size. Consider both to be transparent. Can you place one on top of the other in a way that forms three squares? The resulting squares can be any size.

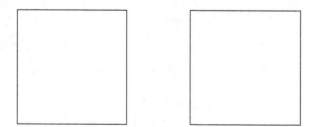

Copyright © 2009 by John Wiley & Sons, Inc.

126. Below is a right angle. It has 90° between the two lines. What would an angle of 180° look like?

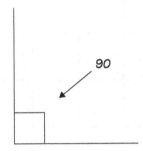

127. If three cubes were glued together as in the illustration below, how many faces would be visible if you picked this stack up and looked at it?

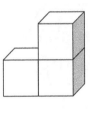

HINT #1
Think of each face having a different picture of your favorite athlete or singer.

HINT #2
How many faces can't be seen?

128. How many sugar cubes are in the illustration below if you know that all sugar cubes are filled in behind the "tower" of sugar cubes in front?

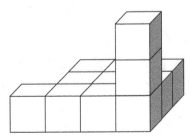

Copyright © 2009 by John Wiley & Sons, Inc.

129. How many squares of any size are in the illustration below?

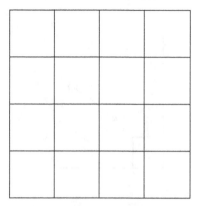

130. Which illustration doesn't belong with the others?

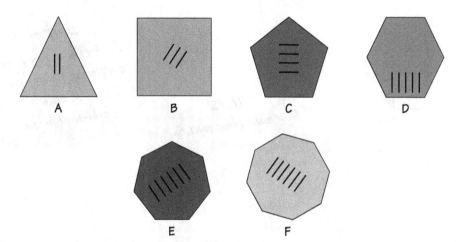

131. Can you rearrange the three triangles below to form a trapezoid? A trapezoid has four sides with two sides parallel to each other.

Copyright © 2009 by John Wiley & Sons, Inc.

Copyright © 2009 by John Wiley & Sons, Inc.

126. Below is a right angle. It has 90° between the two lines. What would an angle of 180° look like?

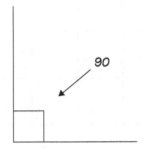

127. If three cubes were glued together as in the illustration below, how many faces would be visible if you picked this stack up and looked at it?

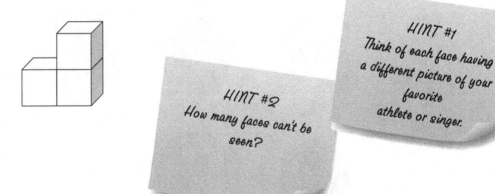

HINT #1
Think of each face having a different picture of your favorite athlete or singer.

HINT #2
How many faces can't be seen?

128. How many sugar cubes are in the illustration below if you know that all sugar cubes are filled in behind the "tower" of sugar cubes in front?

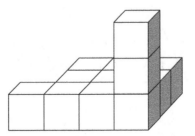

129. How many squares of any size are in the illustration below?

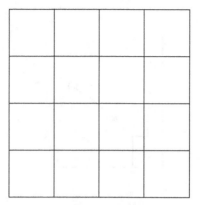

130. Which illustration doesn't belong with the others?

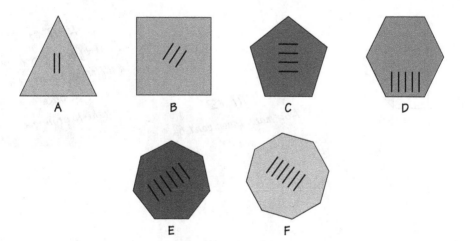

131. Can you rearrange the three triangles below to form a trapezoid? A trapezoid has four sides with two sides parallel to each other.

Copyright © 2009 by John Wiley & Sons, Inc.

132. Can you place the numbers 4 and 5 on the unfolded cube below so that when the cube is folded up, the opposite faces add up to 7?

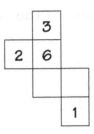

133. How many cubes are in the stack below? All rows and columns finish out their respective row or column—unless you see them end!

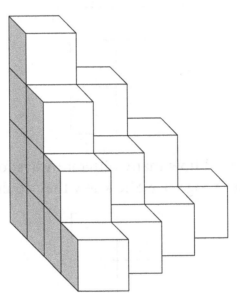

Copyright © 2009 by John Wiley & Sons, Inc.

134. Melinda was continuing to work on the math project for her school. She wanted to show how different shapes would fit together, as well as how the same shapes fit together.

She noticed that two squares of the same size can fit together in only one way, like this:

She then noticed that three squares of the same size can fit together in two different ways:

Then she wondered how many different ways four squares of the same size could fit together. She knew they could fit together like this:

But she wasn't sure how many total ways there were to fit four together. Can you help her?

Copyright © 2009 by John Wiley & Sons, Inc.

135. What comes next in this sequence?

Triangle, Rectangle, Pentagon, Hexagon, ____?____, Octagon, Nonagon

What word comes after Nonagon?

Extra Credit: What is a 12-sided figure called?

Copyright © 2009 by John Wiley & Sons, Inc.

136. Here's what a 90° angle looks like:

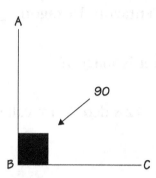

The black square is a symbol for a 90° angle.

An acute angle is an angle less than 90°. Here's what an acute angle looks like:

An obtuse angle is one greater than 90°. Here's what an obtuse angle looks like:

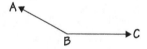

Here are five times you would find on a standard clock. If the times were formed by an hour hand and a minute hand, which two of these times would form an obtuse angle?

1:05   2:00   3:10   6:20   8:00   11:30

Copyright © 2009 by John Wiley & Sons, Inc.

137. How many different angles of any size are in the drawing below?

To get you started, ∠BAE is one angle and ∠CAD is one angle.

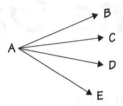

138. In the illustration below, all angles are 90°. Look at the measurements given, and use them to figure out the answers to the following questions.

a. What is the length of A?

b. What is the length of B?

c. What is the length of C?

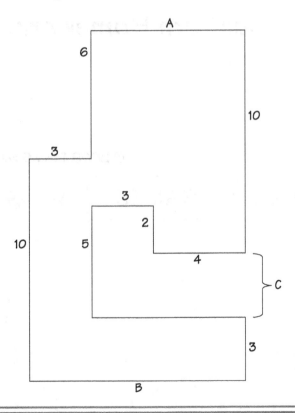

Copyright © 2009 by John Wiley & Sons, Inc.

Just for Fun: Frame Game

139. Find the hidden word or phrase.

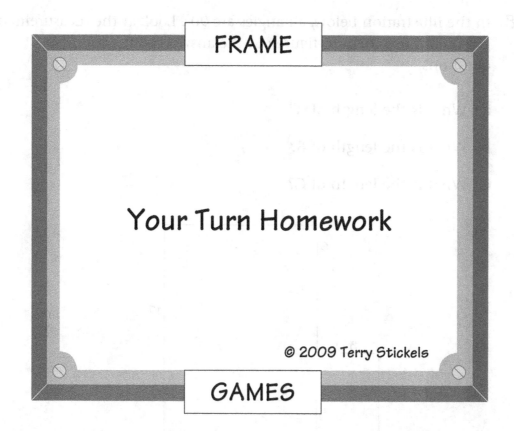

FRAME

Your Turn Homework

© 2009 Terry Stickels

GAMES

140. An old puzzle asks four family members to divide a piece of land into four equal areas. Here is the land:

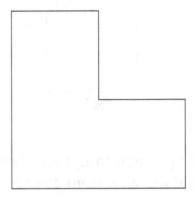

Here's the answer usually given:

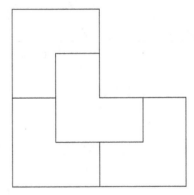

The new puzzle is this: Can you divide the same piece of land into equal areas for two, three, four, or six family members? Here's the catch: Each piece of land must be a triangle.

Copyright © 2009 by John Wiley & Sons, Inc.

141. Below are several views of a pyramid that has four equal sides and a base or bottom.

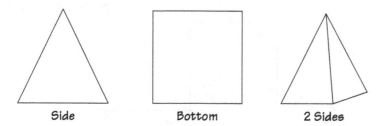

If you looked at this pyramid from high above it, as if you were in an airplane, what would the view from directly above it look like?

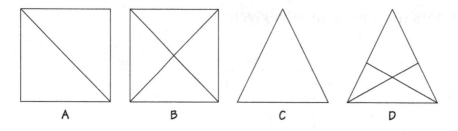

Copyright © 2009 by John Wiley & Sons, Inc.

142. There is an old puzzle that starts with 12 toothpicks arranged into a square like this:

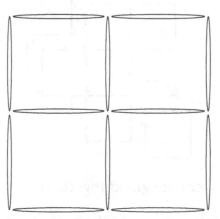

The puzzle is to see how many squares of any size you can make by moving just two of the toothpicks. The usual answer is:

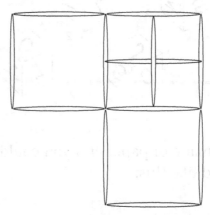

The new puzzle is to start with the same 12 toothpicks—only this time see how many triangles you can create of any size by moving 2 toothpicks! It's okay to place toothpicks on top of one another.

Copyright © 2009 by John Wiley & Sons, Inc.

143. Below are seven 1-inch cubes that are glued together.

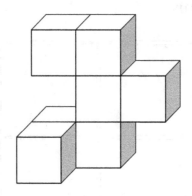

How many total faces are glued together?

144. Here are four different views of the same cube. Six different letters are used: H, J, L, M, O, and S.

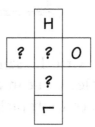

If this cube were made of paper and you could unfold it, the six faces could be displayed like this:

	H	
?	?	O
	?	
	L	

What letters go where the question marks are? How are they oriented? In other words, how do they appear on the face in relation to the other letters?

Copyright © 2009 by John Wiley & Sons, Inc.

145. A square piece of paper is folded in half. The square then is cut into two rectangles along the fold.

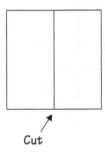

Cut

Regardless of the size of the square, one of the following is always true. Which one?

a. The area of both rectangles is larger than the area of the square.

b. The perimeter of the square is always greater than the perimeters of the rectangles added together.

c. The perimeter of both rectangles together is always $1\frac{1}{2}$ times greater than the perimeter of the square.

d. The area of the square is always three times as large as the area of both rectangles added together.

Copyright © 2009 by John Wiley & Sons, Inc.

146. Here is another cube-folding puzzle. There are 11 ways to unfold a cube. Here are four of those ways:

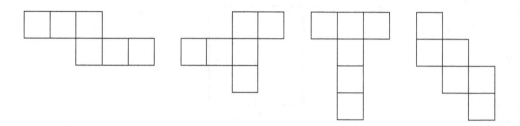

Here are three more ways to unfold a cube. Why only three? One of these patterns will not fold back into a cube. Which one is the odd one out?

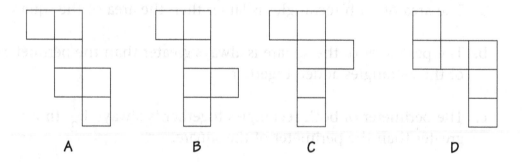

A   B   C   D

147. I am a four-sided, closed figure drawn on paper. My sides are all different lengths, so my angles are different. I answer to two names. What are they?

Copyright © 2009 by John Wiley & Sons, Inc.

148. The following square has two shaded sections representing __?__ of the area of the square.

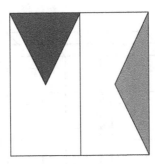

a. $\dfrac{1}{3}$

b. $\dfrac{1}{4}$

c. $\dfrac{3}{8}$

d. $\dfrac{1}{2}$

HINT
You can use a straightedge to check.

149. If you have 7 triangles, 13 squares, 5 hexagons, and 8 pentagons, how many total sides do you have?

Copyright © 2009 by John Wiley & Sons, Inc.

150. The stack of cubes below is the beginning of a 5 × 4 × 3 configuration (60 cubes total). How many more cubes have to be added to complete the project?

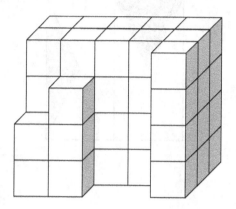

a. 3

b. 8

c. 11

d. 21

Copyright © 2009 by John Wiley & Sons, Inc.

Just for Fun: Frame Game

151. Find the hidden word or phrase.

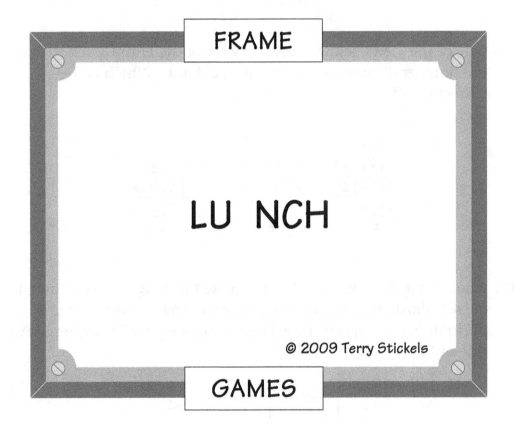

FRAME

LU NCH

© 2009 Terry Stickels

GAMES

152. There are 11 cubes on the bottom layer of the stacked cubes below.

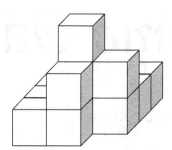

One of the views below is the top view of the entire stack with the number of cubes in each vertical column. Which is the correct view?

1	1	1
1	1	1
1	3	2
1	2	

A

1	1	1	1
2	3	1	1
1	2	1	

B

1	1	2	
1	2	3	2
1	1	1	1

C

153. Below is an illustration called a "squared rectangle." Even though the outside illustration is a rectangle, each of the individual inside illustrations is a square. How large is the A square? How long is each side of B?

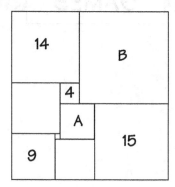

Copyright © 2009 by John Wiley & Sons, Inc.

154. Look at the seven lettered polygons pictured here.

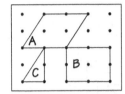 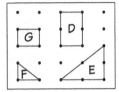

In the puzzles below, two or more of the seven illustrations are put together as in the two examples shown. See if you can determine which polygons make up each illustration by placing a letter in each polygon.

Example #1   Example #2

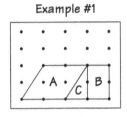 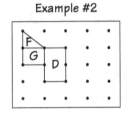

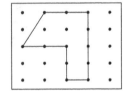 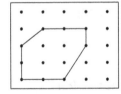 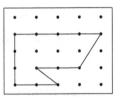

155. One cube is missing from the bottom layer of this stack of cubes. (It's hidden from view by the tall column.) How many total individual cubes are in the entire stack of cubes?

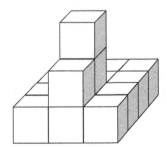

Copyright © 2009 by John Wiley & Sons, Inc.

156. The top view of this stack of cubes would look like which of the diagrams below?

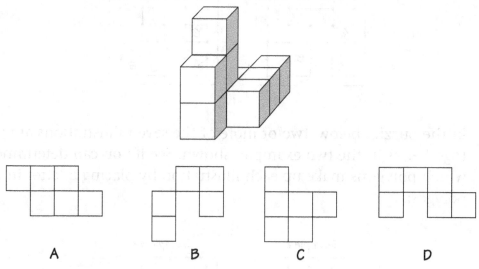

A   B   C   D

157. *Add up my sides*
And what do you see?

A number that's easy
A multiple of 3.

So please pay attention.
Please take heed.

Look at Figure C.
What do I need?

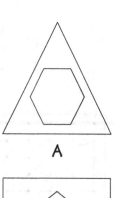

A

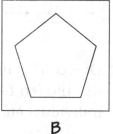

B

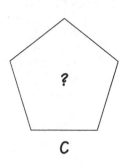

C

Copyright © 2009 by John Wiley & Sons, Inc.

158. This type of puzzle is called a Stickpath. You compare the length of path AB to the length of path YZ in each box. It's fun to pick teams and see who can come up with the answers the fastest. The idea is to try to determine which line is longer in each box. (Each horizontal and vertical line segment is the same length. The diagonal line segments are slightly longer but the same length in each box.)

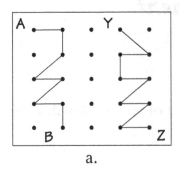

a.

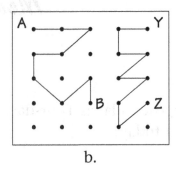

b.

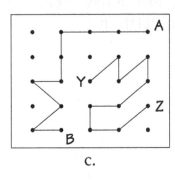

c.

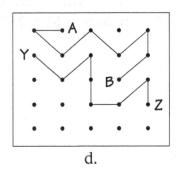

d.

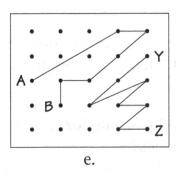

e.

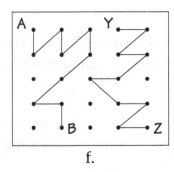

f.

Copyright © 2009 by John Wiley & Sons, Inc.

Copyright © 2009 by John Wiley & Sons, Inc.

Measurement

159. Suppose today is Thursday. What day of the week will it be 19 days from today?

160. The number of days from October 13 to November 26 (including the 13th and the 26th) *divided by* the number of days from May 28 to June 11 (including May 28th and June 11th) is:

a. 10

b. 8

c. 5

d. 3

161. John is measuring a banner for the school play and needs to know how many inches are in 5 yards and 2 feet. Can you help him out?

162. You went to bed last night at 9:15 and woke up for school this morning at 6:45. How long did you sleep?

163. 11 hours ago it was the morning. 3 hours from now will be 1 AM tomorrow. What time was it in the morning I first mentioned?

164. A strange far-off land called Zooplo uses a system of measurement similar to ours. Plus, this country has other units of measure that fit with ours. Here's an example:

Zooplo uses inches, feet, and yards: 12 inches equals 1 foot, and 3 feet equals 1 yard. But Zooplo also has a unit of measure called a Zoop: 3 yards = 1 Zoop.

Here's what I need to know: How many inches are in 3 Zoops?

165. Today is Thursday. I came home from a trip 3 days before the day after last Monday. How many days have I been home?

a. 1 day

b. 2 days

c. 6 days

d. Can't tell from the clues

166. A grandfather clock chimes on the hour and on the half hour. The difference is that the chime on the hour has the same number of chimes as the hour, but the chime on the half hour chimes only once. For example, at 8 o'clock the clock will chime eight times. At 8:30 the clock chimes only once. How many total chimes are there starting from 12 o'clock noon to 7 o'clock PM?

Copyright © 2009 by John Wiley & Sons, Inc.

167. A ruler is marked off in $\frac{1}{16}$-inch sections. Mary measures 2 ft. 3 in. How many $\frac{1}{16}$-inch markings are in 2 ft. 3 in.?

168. A wooden block is 3 inches long, 3 inches wide, and 1 inch high. The block is painted gray on all six sides.

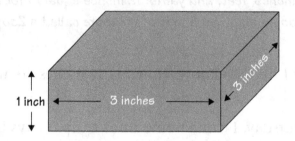

Then the block is cut into nine 1-inch cubes.

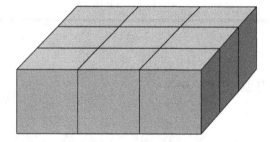

How many of the small cubes have only two sides painted gray?

Copyright © 2009 by John Wiley & Sons, Inc.

169. Below is a mobile hanging from the ceiling in a museum. One of the students in a group looking at the exhibits asked, "I wonder how much that last box weighs?"

Her friend replied, "I'm not sure, but I think it has to do with the length and weight on one side of the mobile being exactly the same as the length and weight on the other side."

A third student agreed. "Yes. My brother told me you have to multiply the length by the weight on one side, and that equals the length times the weight on the other side."

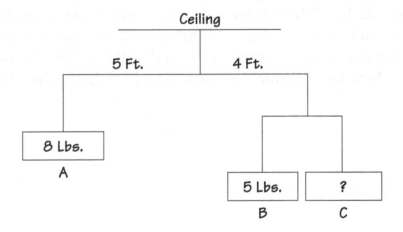

So how much weight should be in box C?

170. If 1 cent is equal to 1 second, how much money would you have after 3 minutes and 37 seconds? How much money would you have in 4 hours and 13 minutes? How much money would you have after 1 day?

Copyright © 2009 by John Wiley & Sons, Inc.

171. Emilio was helping one of his teachers clean up the chemistry lab at school. He was supposed to wash a 5-liter container and a 4-liter container when the teacher said, "I can't find the 3-liter container, and I need exactly that amount to mix with the cleaning fluid. I suppose I'll have to guess how much to pour in the bucket."

Emilio said, "Don't worry. I'll bring you exactly 3 liters from these two containers I have. Just give me a few seconds to move the water back and forth between the two containers to give you the 3 liters." How did Emilio accomplish this?

172. You're making a banner for your friend Melanie's 11th birthday. The banner is 40 inches long. You have to center the name "Melanie" in the middle of the banner and have 1 inch between each of the letters. Each of the 7 letters is 4 inches wide. How much room will be on each end of her name to the end of the banner? In other words, how far is it from the letter M to the edge of the banner?

Copyright © 2009 by John Wiley & Sons, Inc.

Just for Fun: Frame Game

173. Find the hidden word or phrase.

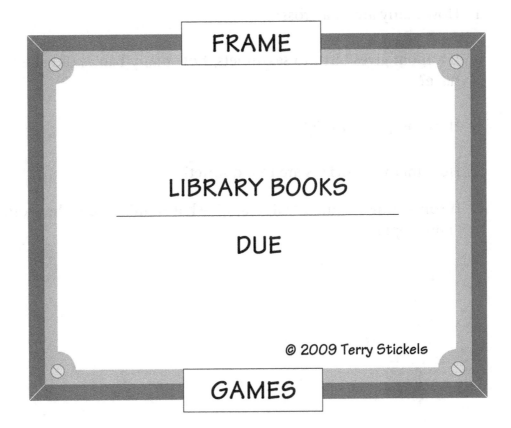

FRAME

LIBRARY BOOKS

_____

DUE

© 2009 Terry Stickels

GAMES

174. If 1 inch = 2.54 centimeters, then 1 yard is = ___ meters?

175. You may know that a "baker's dozen" is 13 (if you order a dozen doughnuts, for example, an extra doughnut may be thrown in, free of charge). You also may know that a "score" is 20, as in President Abraham Lincoln's Gettysburg Address, "Four score and seven years ago," which is 87 years. But can you tell me:

a. How many are in a gross?

b. If a mom gives birth to sextuplets, how many babies did she have?

c. How long is a fortnight?

d. How many musicians are in a quintet?

e. If something weighs a "kilogram," what number does the word "kilo" represent?

Copyright © 2009 by John Wiley & Sons, Inc.

176. What's the final number in this poem?

The pounds in a ton
Times the sides of a square.

Now that's a good start.
Do you think it is fair?

Divide by the pints
In a quart, don't you see?
This isn't hard.
Now add 33.

Add in the days
of a year with a leap.

Let's keep it fun.
Don't want you to sleep!

We'll add a few more
Not too many, you'll see.
Let's keep it simple...
Add 12 minus 3.

So tell me, my friends,
How did you do?

Did I make it too easy
For whiz kids like you?

Copyright © 2009 by John Wiley & Sons, Inc.

177. A flagpole of 20 feet casts a shadow of 5 feet. If the flagpole were only 12 feet high, how long would its shadow be?

178. Look at the series of clocks below.

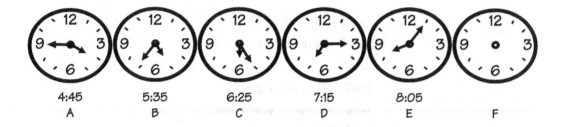

| 4:45 | 5:35 | 6:25 | 7:15 | 8:05 | |
| A | B | C | D | E | F |

The time on clock "F" will most likely be:

a. 9:00

b. 9:05

c. 8:55

d. 11:00

Copyright © 2009 by John Wiley & Sons, Inc.

179. Anthony and Mario can cut their uncle's lawn in 3 hours. The total area of the lawn is 900 square yards. Behind their uncle's house is a small strip of grass that measures 900 square feet. If the boys can cut a 900-square-yard lawn in 3 hours, how long will it take them to mow 900 square feet?

HINT
Be careful—you're dealing with both yards and feet.

180. Caitlin's uncle is a football referee who refs a game seven days a week during the season. Because of his schedule, he can take his striped shirts to the cleaners only one day a week. He takes them in on Monday and picks them up on Tuesday. If he wears a different striped shirt every day of the week, what is the fewest number of shirts he would need to make it through the season?

Copyright © 2009 by John Wiley & Sons, Inc.

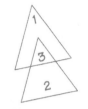

Part III

MATHEMATICAL REASONING

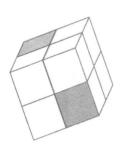

Visual

181. Below are nine dots arranged in a grid. Your goal is to connect as many of the dots as possible without lifting your pencil off the paper and without crossing any lines you have already drawn. All lines must be straight, and no diagonal lines are allowed. How many lines can you draw?

Example:

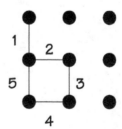

Copyright © 2009 by John Wiley & Sons, Inc.

182. Our friend, Moolie the mouse, is about to enter a maze where each block has a rule on how to proceed.

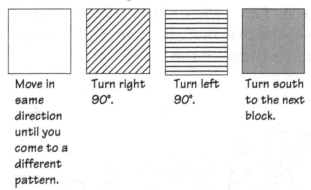

Move in same direction until you come to a different pattern.

Turn right 90°.

Turn left 90°.

Turn south to the next block.

Moolie the mouse is going to enter moving from left to right at block C. The directions are from the mouse's view. If the directions tell you to leave a box in a certain direction, depart from the box in the middle. That is, if you have to turn, turn in the middle of the box to leave.

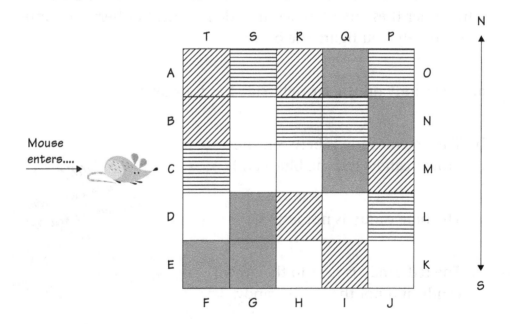

What is the letter of the box where Moolie will exit?

Copyright © 2009 by John Wiley & Sons, Inc.

183. Below are three stacks of Frisbees. The first stack has six, the second stack has four, and the third stack has two. How many moves would it take to create four stacks of three Frisbees each from the three stacks below? You may move as many Frisbees from any stack to any other stack to accomplish this.

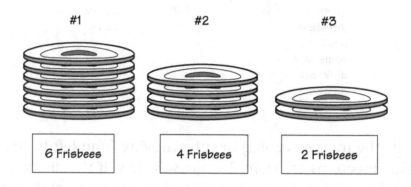

#1   #2   #3

6 Frisbees   4 Frisbees   2 Frisbees

184. I have five different pieces of candy sitting side by side. They are colored blue, brown, pink, green, and red. You don't know in what order these five candies are side by side, but here are some clues to help you figure the order.

a. The candy on the far right side has four letters.

b. The green candy is between the brown candy and the blue candy.

HINT
Making a chart can help you organize the clues.

c. The blue candy is not last.

d. The red candy is next to the brown candy and not the fourth candy.

What is the order of the candies from left to right?

Copyright © 2009 by John Wiley & Sons, Inc.

185. Six coins are arranged as shown below. Can you move one coin to make a cross with four coins in each row?

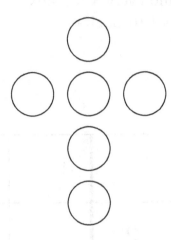

186. One of the most interesting and fun branches of mathematics is the study of game theory. The theories of playing and solving games are studied by mathematicians worldwide—even games as seemingly simple as Tic-Tac-Toe! Below is the start of a game in which the O has moved first. You are the X, and it's your turn to move. The challenge is to place your X in the square that will stop the O from winning the game. (Of course, to win a game, a player has to have three X's or three O's in a row, column, or diagonal.) Where does your X go?

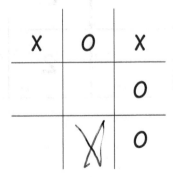

Copyright © 2009 by John Wiley & Sons, Inc.

187. Sudoku is a type of math game that many people enjoy. Fill in the grid so that every row, every column, and every 3 × 2 box contains the numbers 1 through 6.

HINT

There is only one solution.

4	5	6	1	3	2
1	3	2	4	6	5
6	1	3	5	2	3
3	2	5	6	4	1
2	6	1	3	5	4
5	4	3	2	1	6

Copyright © 2009 by John Wiley & Sons, Inc.

Just for Fun: Frame Game

188. Find the hidden word or phrase.

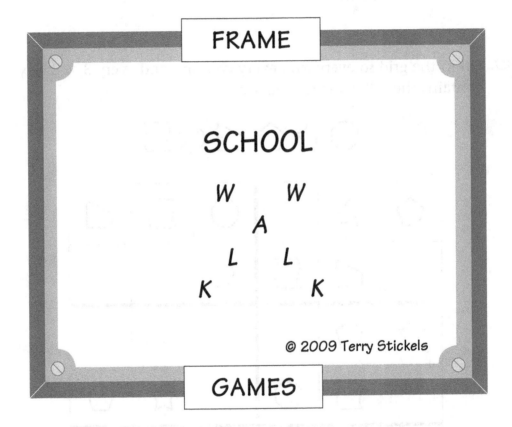

189. Three of the four illustrations below can be formed without lifting your pencil off the page and without crossing any other lines. One illustration cannot be created without lifting your pencil off the page. Which one?

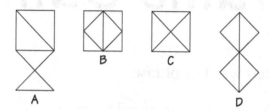

190. Fill in the grid so every row, every column, and every 3 × 2 box contains the following six shapes:

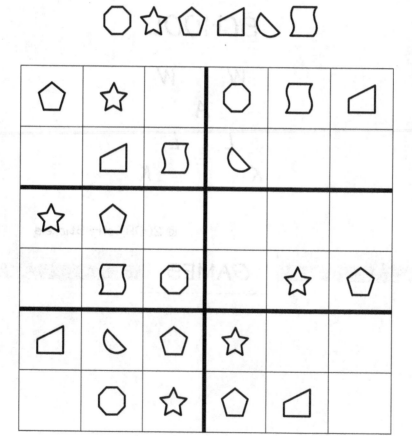

Copyright © 2009 by John Wiley & Sons, Inc.

191. Below is a 3 × 3 grid where the center square is blacked out and not in play. Using the numbers 1 through 8 once and only once, can you place the numbers in such a way that no two consecutive numbers are next to each other, including the short diagonals, as noted by the four arrows?

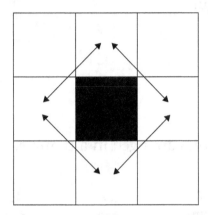

192. Can you move or remove three of the toothpicks and end up with three squares?

193. Using two triangles of the same size, how many different triangles of any size can you make? Here is an example:

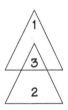

Can you see the three triangles in the figure above? Now can you place two triangles together to get more than three? What is the maximum number of triangles you can make with two triangles?

Copyright © 2009 by John Wiley & Sons, Inc.

194. Now try this: Can you take two triangles of the same size and put them together in such a way that the intersection of the two triangles creates one four-sided figure?

HINT
The figure might look like something you would see on a man wearing a tuxedo.

195. Below are six pennies arranged in a triangle.

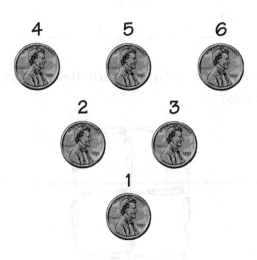

Here's the challenge: Turn this triangle upside down by changing the positions of only two coins!

Copyright © 2009 by John Wiley & Sons, Inc.

Just for Fun: Frame Game

196. Find the hidden word or phrase.

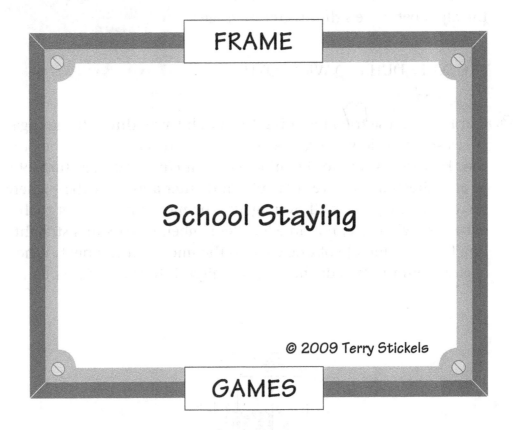

FRAME

School Staying

© 2009 Terry Stickels

GAMES

Copyright © 2009 by John Wiley & Sons, Inc.

197. Some of the most fun puzzles to solve are cryptograms. They've been around in many forms for ages.

"Crypto" is a Greek word meaning "secret." "Gram" is a Greek root meaning "message." So you have "secret message."

Here's a cryptogram. See if you can decipher the code and come up with the message. This is called a "shift cipher." I'm merely shifting the letters in the alphabet. Here's the "secret message."

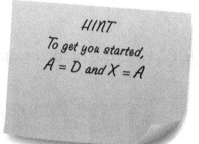

HINT
To get you started,
A = D and X = A

SXCCOHV DUH IXQ WR VROYH!

198. Our little mouse friend is going to work his way through the sugar cubes shown below. He can enter any cube he chooses on the bottom row. He eats his way to the middle of that cube and then turns 90° in any direction to leave that cube and enter another cube—where he repeats the process all over again. The mouse must enter each cube through a face, not an edge. Remember, he eats in a straight line from the middle of one cube to the middle of the next. When he begins from the outside, he enters straight into the middle of a face.

The shaded cubes are diagonal from each other.

What is the least number of cubes the mouse has to eat through to move from one cube on the bottom to that cube's diagonal cube on top? Is it possible for him to eat through all eight cubes?

199. Which one of the illustrations below is different from the rest? Why?

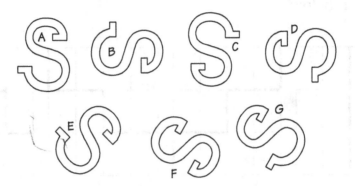

200. Ellis, Mary, and Peter were trying to put three batteries into a handheld game. They couldn't read or tell which way the batteries were supposed to go in. They couldn't even see which end was positive (+) or which end was negative (−). Ellis said, "There's no reason to panic. All we have to do is try the twelve different ways the batteries can fit in there, and we'll be right on one of the ways." Mary said, "We won't have to try twelve ways. It can be done in fewer ways than that." Peter chimed in, "I know who's right, and I can show a simple picture to prove it."

Who's right? Can you draw a quick picture or diagram to show the answer?

201. Below are two circles of the same size intersecting each other. As you can see, two circles can intersect each other to create three interior sections.

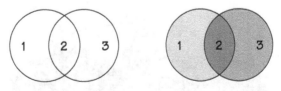

If three circles of the same size intersect each other, how many different sections could be created inside the circles?

Copyright © 2009 by John Wiley & Sons, Inc.

202. Tyler and Toni are preparing some posters for their classroom's math exhibit for the parents. They have 12 pieces of paper divided in half as shown below.

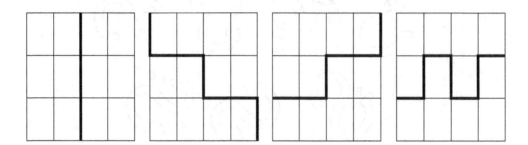

When they showed their designs to Tamika, they told her that they were finished showing how a figure with 12 squares could be divided in half. Since these were the only ways the sheets could be divided, they were going to color their work and post it on the wall.

Tamika replied, "You might want to think about this. I think there may be at least one more way to divide the 12 sheets of paper." Was Tamika right? Are there other ways to do this?

203. Below is a top view of three large brownies. Phillip's dad left these for Phillip and two friends, but three friends came home from school with him. Is there a way you can help Phillip figure out how all four can divide the three brownies equally among them?

Copyright © 2009 by John Wiley & Sons, Inc.

Just for Fun: Frame Game

204. Find the hidden word or phrase.

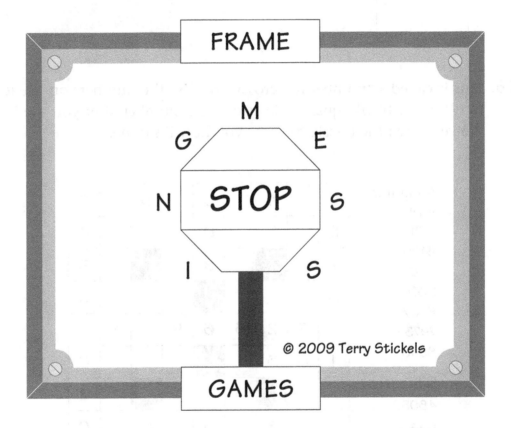

205. Add two more straight lines to the illustration below to make two more squares.

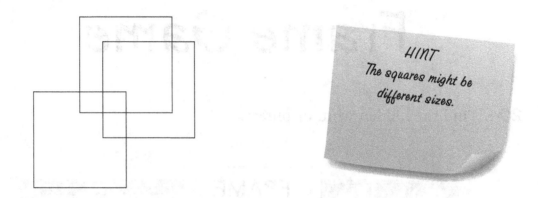

HINT
The squares might be different sizes.

206. This is called a "number fit" crossword. Use the numbers on the left to fill in the blank squares. Cross off each number after you use it. We've started the puzzle to show you how it's done.

4 Figures
~~1031~~
1521
~~2495~~
3089
5206
~~6207~~
~~7973~~
8545

5 Figures
48958
59617

7 Figures
3241030
~~7266901~~
8007084

7		4	3		8	2
9		5	0		1	4
7	■		9	■		9
3			■			5
	7	2	6	6	9	0	1
1	0	3	1	■			6
	■		7		■		2
		1	5		6	0
		6	6		3	7

Copyright © 2009 by John Wiley & Sons, Inc.

207. How many squares of any size are in this illustration?

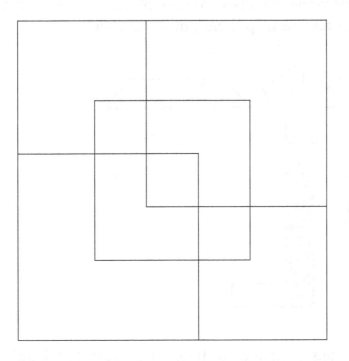

HINT
Be careful. There may be more than you think!

208. One of the illustrations below does not belong with the others because of the way it is designed. Which illustration is the odd one out? Why?

HINT
Look for simple, basic characteristics.

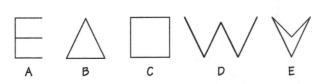

A   B   C   D   E

Copyright © 2009 by John Wiley & Sons, Inc.

209. Below are the pieces of a banner used to form an L for Latin Club. The problem is that someone forgot to mark the pieces to show Kelsey and Alex how to put them together. Here are the pieces, and also what the L should look like. Can you help them put it together?

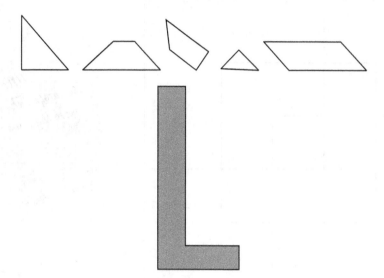

210. A triangle has no diagonals. A square has two. A pentagon has 5 and a hexagon has 9 diagonals. How many diagonals would an octagon have? A dodecagon?

Here's a picture of a pentagon and its 5 diagonals.

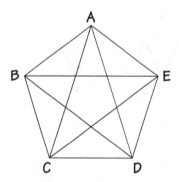

Here we have a pentagon ABCDE. The diagonals are:

AC   AD   BD   BE   CE

Copyright © 2009 by John Wiley & Sons, Inc.

211. Lindsay is playing in a fall softball league with a short schedule. There are only five teams, and each team can play the other teams once and only once. How many total games will be played in this league for the fall season?

How many games would be played if there were only three teams? Four teams? Look for a relationship between the number and total games.

How many games with eight teams?

212. The soccer club is putting together a mural using lightly colored transparent paper. This paper then is cut into squares of different sizes that are placed next to each other to make the designs for the mural. Of course, the club wants to save money, so its members are trying to buy the minimum number of sheets of colored paper. Below is one of the designs they are going to use. What is the minimum number of squares they will need to make this design?

Note: Remember—the squares are transparent, and it's not important which colors go next to each other. Also, different sizes of squares will be used.

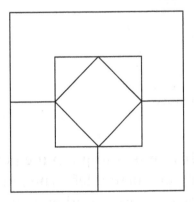

Copyright © 2009 by John Wiley & Sons, Inc.

213. Here's a fun game to try with family and friends. Take 10 pennies and arrange them like this:

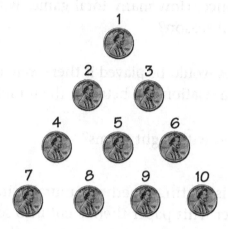

Remove penny number 9 to make a space. Now the remaining pennies can "jump" over one another.

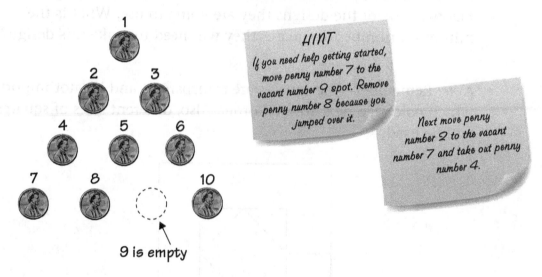

9 is empty

HINT
If you need help getting started, move penny number 7 to the vacant number 9 spot. Remove penny number 8 because you jumped over it.

Next move penny number 2 to the vacant number 7 and take out penny number 4.

The challenge in this game is to jump the pennies one at a time so there is only one penny left. The jumps are just like checkers—jump one coin over another coin and into an empty space. Then remove the penny that you just jumped over.

Copyright © 2009 by John Wiley & Sons, Inc.

214. Joey and Jenny are twins having a birthday party. Their mom made them a round chocolate cake. Eight kids total (including Joey and Jenny) will be eating the cake, and they want to make sure that everyone gets the same amount. Jenny said to her mom, "I'm going to cut the cake with just three slices—the first to cut it in half, the second to cut it in fourths, and then I'll stack those four pieces on top of each other and make one slice through all of them." Jenny's mom replied, "Please don't try that. There will be cake crumbs all over the place, not to mention the difficulty of stacking four pieces of cake on top of one another. There's another way to cut the cake in eight even pieces using just three slices of the knife." Can you help Joey and Jenny cut the cake neatly with only three slices?

Copyright © 2009 by John Wiley & Sons, Inc.

215. Try your hand at these four Sudokus.

#1

	1		4	3	9		6	
6	8							
						4	5	
				8				2
	6		1	5	2		9	
2			3					
	2	8						
						4	7	
	4		9	2	5		1	

#2

					5		4	6
				7			5	
3		4		1				
7	6		1					4
		5		3		8		
4				7			2	1
			9			6		3
	1			5				
2	4		3					

#3

			4		7	8		
		2		5				
			9	8	7		6	
2	8							5
	1					8		
6						2	1	
1		5	6	3				
			4		2			
		4	1		9			

#4

	6			2				7
					8			1
	7		4				5	
		1		8	9			
6	5						8	3
			6	1		2		
	1				7		9	
4			5					
5				6			7	

216. The letters around the boxes below are arranged in an orderly way that spell out a question. Can you find the letter that goes where the question mark is, and figure out what it says?

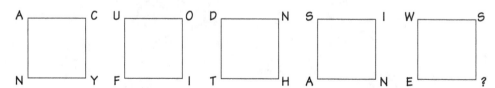

Copyright © 2009 by John Wiley & Sons, Inc.

Just for Fun: Frame Game

217. Find the hidden word or phrase.

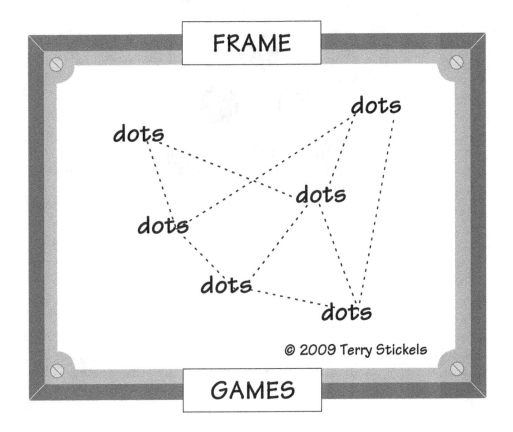

© 2009 Terry Stickels

218. Place six pennies in the arrangement shown below. You're going to play a game in which you and a friend will take turns picking up these pennies. The goal of the game is to leave your opponent with one single penny. The rules are simple: You can pick up as many pennies as you want on your turn—as long as the pennies are in the same row and the pennies are next to each other. In other words, you can pick up the first and second pennies in the third row, or the second and third pennies in that row, but you can't pick up the first and the last pennies in the third row on the same turn. In order to win, is it better to go first or second?

Copyright © 2009 by John Wiley & Sons, Inc.

219. What letter is to the left of the letter that is two letters below the letter three letters to the right of the letter above the letter K?

A	B	C	D	E
F	G	H	I	J
K	L	M	N	O
P	Q	R	S	T
U	V	W	X	Y

Copyright © 2009 by John Wiley & Sons, Inc.

220. Can you find your way through these two mazes?

Start

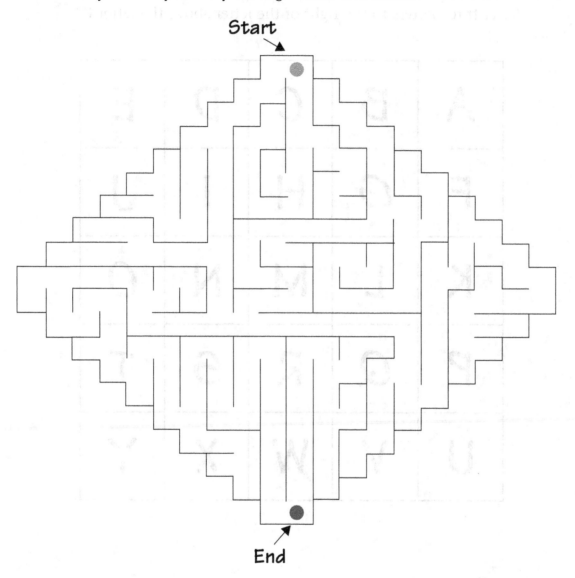

End

Copyright © 2009 by John Wiley & Sons, Inc.

Start

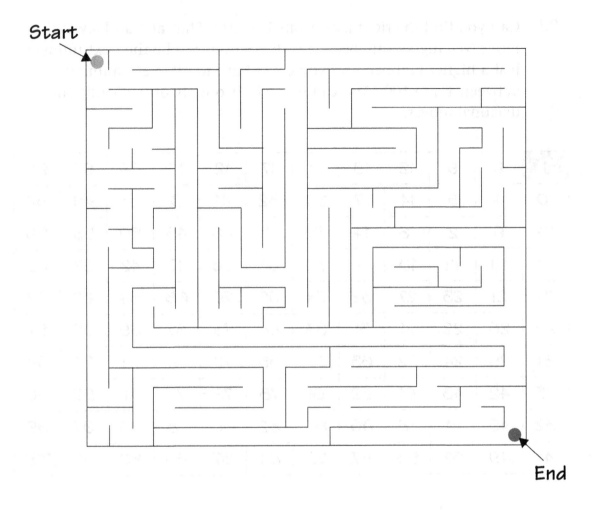

End

Copyright © 2009 by John Wiley & Sons, Inc.

221. Can you find the right path from 1 to 100? Start at 1 and always move to a higher number. (This doesn't have to be the next number, just a higher number. And you don't have to hit every number between 1 and 100.) You can move horizontally or vertically—no diagonal moves.

1	6	9	12	19	21	17	12	10	54	57	60
10	4	5	14	17	30	32	41	8	51	49	52
13	6	2	16	14	15	43	46	49	50	53	56
17	19	12	18	17	35	37	36	43	42	57	60
15	21	23	27	32	34	32	70	68	64	62	59
28	26	22	21	31	33	44	73	67	69	60	57
31	25	24	32	63	67	65	72	75	72	73	84
35	42	43	61	62	61	78	79	77	71	82	80
32	45	41	58	86	83	82	80	78	93	97	99
41	49	52	56	87	79	84	87	89	90	88	100

Copyright © 2009 by John Wiley & Sons, Inc.

222. Each series below follows its own logical rules. Can you determine the next in each series?

a.

$?$

67 56

36 31 25

20 16 15 10

11 9 7 8 2

4 7 2 5 3 1

b. 3Z 4Y 5X 6W 7V 8U ?

c. 7 12 11 16 15 20 19 ?

d.

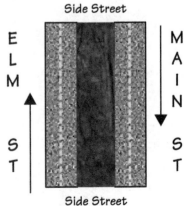

223. Michelle likes to ride her bike up Elm St. and then come back home on Main St. Both streets appear to be the same length from an airplane view, but remember—that's only one perspective. She rides at exactly the same speed every day, and the speed is the same for both Elm St. and Main St. Yet it always takes her longer coming back on Main St. What could be a reason for this?

Side Street

E L M S T

M A I N S T

Side Street

Copyright © 2009 by John Wiley & Sons, Inc.

224. Below is a grid with nine different shapes in various locations. Can you place each of the nine shapes into the four areas of the grid so that none of the shapes are duplicated in any of the rows across or down?

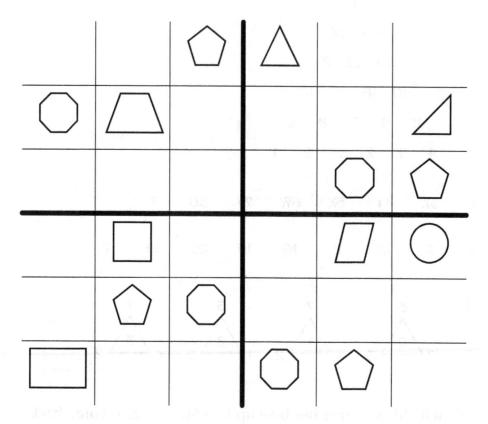

Copyright © 2009 by John Wiley & Sons, Inc.

225. Cale was creating a game in which the players would start in the lower left-hand corner of a board made of squares. They eventually would end up in the upper right-hand corner of the last and highest square (if the squares were stacked on top of each other). You can move only up or left to right to reach the finish. Cale knows that he can take three separate paths with three squares (example below). He's trying to figure out how many paths he can take if there were six squares. Can you help him out?

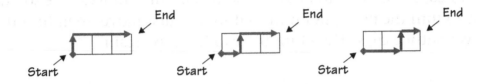

How many different paths with six squares?

226. Here's a little fun with the digits 1–9. The key here is to keep an open mind and let it be flexible. What comes next?

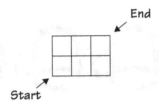

a.

b.

c.

Copyright © 2009 by John Wiley & Sons, Inc.

227. An old puzzle asks you to set three cups as follows:

The goal is to turn all three cups into the "up" position by moving two cups at a time. You have to do this in three moves. The solution is to turn the two cups on the left for the first move, then turn the two outside cups. Then turn the two left cups again.

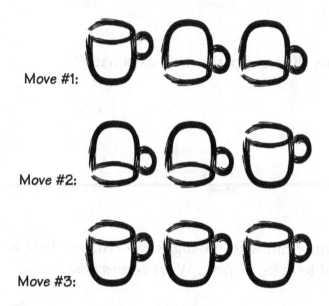

Move #1:

Move #2:

Move #3:

Here's the new puzzle. Use four cups set up like this:

Now move all four cups into an upright position in exactly three moves, moving two cups at a time.

Copyright © 2009 by John Wiley & Sons, Inc.

228. Is it possible to draw three straight lines through the square below so there is only one circle in each of the sections created by the lines?

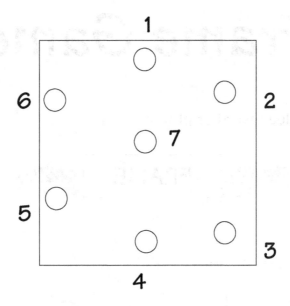

229. The goal of this next puzzle is to exchange the positions of the penny and the nickel and end up with the quarters in boxes 4 and 6 in the least number of moves. You can move only to an adjacent space, and you cannot move diagonally. How many moves does it take?

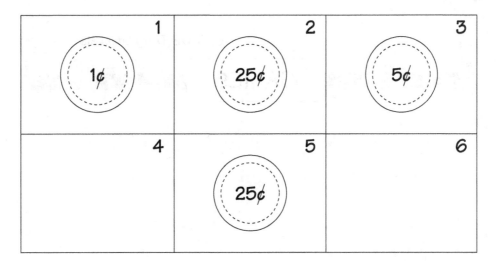

Copyright © 2009 by John Wiley & Sons, Inc.

Just for Fun: Frame Game

230. Find the hidden word or phrase.

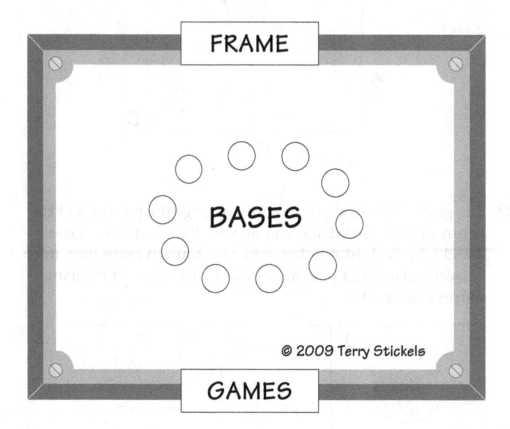

FRAME

BASES

© 2009 Terry Stickels

GAMES

231. Can you trace the following illustration without going over any lines twice? You have to start at A and go to B before you go to C, but you can end the circuit anywhere. Now go on to the illustrations below. Some of them cannot be traced. Just mark "No" on those.

Example:

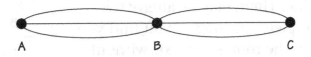

One solution:

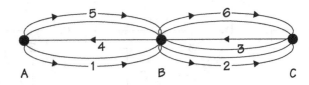

Try these:

a.
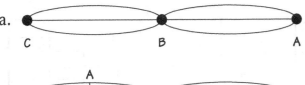

b.
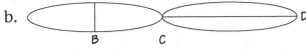

c.
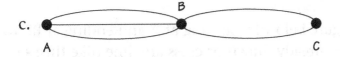

d.
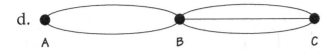

Copyright © 2009 by John Wiley & Sons, Inc.

232. See if you can draw a path that enters and exits each of the lettered rooms in the following floor plans. You must start at A, but you can go through the rooms in any order, even leave the inside of a house and re-enter through a different door. Your path may only go through a door one time, it cannot cross a previous path, and must still be able to exit to the outside. There may be alternative ways to complete the loop. If you find you can't visit all the rooms and exit without violating the rules, just mark CBD, for Can't Be Done. Here's an example:

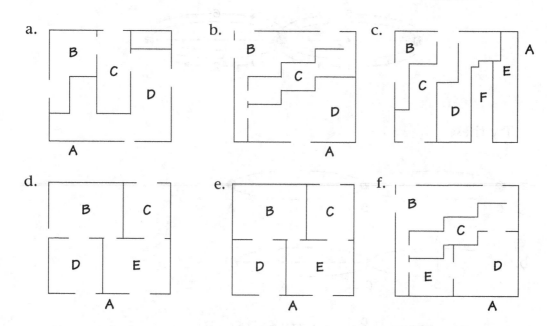

233. Can you retrace the figure below by starting at A and ending at B? You cannot retrace any line already drawn or cross any line (like this: +).

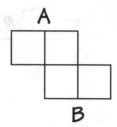

Copyright © 2009 by John Wiley & Sons, Inc.

Other

234. The capital letters in this puzzle share a common characteristic that is not found in the other capital letters in the alphabet. It has to do with the way the letters are constructed and how we see them. What unusual characteristic is shared by these letters?

AHIMOTUVWX

235. What is the next letter in the sequence below?

A B D O P Q ?

HINT #1
Look at how the letters are formed.

HINT #2
The missing letter is the last letter that fits the pattern.

Copyright © 2009 by John Wiley & Sons, Inc.

236. The sum of the dots on opposite faces of one die is always the same. The picture below shows two normal die. How many dots are on the face opposite the face with four dots? All dice have six faces.

237. I have three 3-cent candies and four 5-cent candies. How many different amounts of candy can be made using different combinations of candies?

a. 10 different ways

b. 13 different ways

c. 15 different ways

d. 19 different ways

238. Molly and Maggie have the last names of Ryan and Reilly, but I can never remember if it's Molly Ryan and Maggie Reilly or Molly Reilly and Maggie Ryan. I do know that two of the following statements are false. Given that information, what are the correct full names of each?

• Molly's last name is Ryan.

• Molly's last name is Reilly.

• Maggie's last name is Reilly.

Copyright © 2009 by John Wiley & Sons, Inc.

239. Solve the puzzle using the clues. Fill in the chart using Y for yes or N for no, to help you figure out who ate how many slices of pizza at the pizza party.

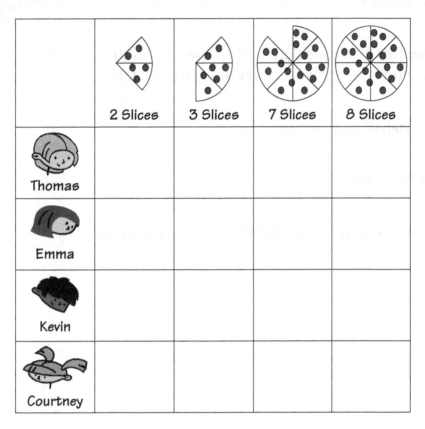

	2 Slices	3 Slices	7 Slices	8 Slices
Thomas				
Emma				
Kevin				
Courtney				

The Story

Four people ate pizza. One person had two slices, one person had three slices, one person had seven slices, and one person had eight slices. Can you figure out how many slices each person ate?

The Clues

1. Kevin ate more than three slices of pizza.

2. Emma ate fewer than eight slices of pizza.

3. Thomas ate more than three slices of pizza.

4. Courtney ate fewer than eight slices of pizza.

5. Emma ate more than two slices of pizza.

6. Thomas ate fewer than eight slices of pizza.

Copyright © 2009 by John Wiley & Sons, Inc.

240. Decode this number puzzle to reveal what it says.

16 21 26 26 12 5 19   1 18 5   1   8 15 15 20!

241. If the first two statements below are true, is the last statement, called a conclusion, true or false?

All baseball players have a bat.

Bob has a bat.

Therefore, Bob is most definitely a baseball player.

Copyright © 2009 by John Wiley & Sons, Inc.

Just for Fun:
Frame Game

242. Find the hidden word or phrase.

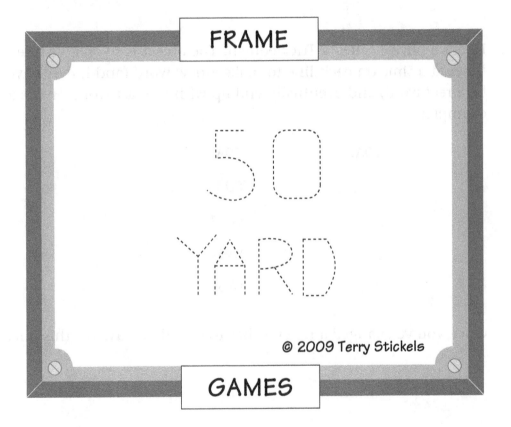

FRAME

50

YARD

© 2009 Terry Stickels

GAMES

243. Marci bought three new T-shirts for summer. She planned to wear them with three different pairs of shorts and two different pairs of sandals. How many different ways can Marci dress for summer?

HINT
First find out the combinations of shorts and T-shirts,

then multiply that by 2 to include the two pairs of sandals.

244. Here's a puzzle called a Trickledown. The object is to change one letter at a time on each line to make a new word (and it *does* have to be a real word) and eventually end up with the last word. Here's an example:

COAT	COAT
_____	COST
_____	CAST
_____	VAST
VASE	VASE

Once you've changed a letter, it has to stay that way. Try this one:

POST

_____

_____

_____

CARE

Copyright © 2009 by John Wiley & Sons, Inc.

245. Brad is taller than Barb. Barb is shorter than Sharon. Sharon is taller than Sally. Sally is not the shortest. If Brad is not next to Sally in height, what is the order of these four friends from tallest to shortest?

246. Can you think of a situation where eighty always comes before seventy? This is not a trick, and it has nothing to do with reversing or counting backward. It has a legitimate answer.

HINT
In this situation, it also comes before forty, fifty, and sixty!

247. Below is a sequence of letters arranged in a logical sequence known to almost everyone. What is the next letter?

S   S   F   T   W   T   <u>?</u>

Copyright © 2009 by John Wiley & Sons, Inc.

248. Here is a crossword puzzle that uses mathematical terms. Have fun using the clues to fill in the grids with the appropriate terms from the word boxes.

Copyright © 2009 by John Wiley & Sons, Inc.

ACROSS

1. Number of sides in a triskaidecagon
5. Any figure having only two dimensions
7. Graph-paper feature
8. Square, for one
10. Angle
12. Private instructor in math
14. You solve math problems with it
15. $\dfrac{7}{4}$ or $\dfrac{12}{31}$
18. Calculation using the – symbol
19. Some amount of
20. A dime _____ ten cents
23. Seven is _____ eight
26. It may be square
27. Six-sided figure
28. Adding machine key

DOWN

1. Multiplication term
2. Prefix for angle
3. Kinds of schools where advanced math may be taught
4. French mathematician René
6. Kind of triangle
7. High school subject
8. Kind of geometry
9. Computer circuitry
11. Math power
13. Height times width
16. Extending from one edge of a solid figure to an opposite edge
17. Get an A+ in math
21. Group of related numbers
22. Decimal dot
23. The trace of a moving point
24. Calculation using the + symbol
25. Line of a graph

ACROSS

THIRTEEN
ANY
EQUALS
GRID
HEXAGON
LESS THAN
MINUS
PENCIL
PLUS
POLYGON
RATIO
ROOT
SLOPE
SURFACE
TUTOR

DOWN

TIMES
DESCARTES
GEOMETRY
LOGIC
MAGNETS
PLANE
RIGHT
TRI
SERIES
AREA
EARN
POINT
SUM
AXIS
EXPONENT
LINE
DIAGONAL

Copyright © 2009 by John Wiley & Sons, Inc.

249. What might be a reasonable two-letter sequence that fits in this puzzle?

HINT
You might know this sequence if you've ever sent a letter.

RI   SC   SD   TN   TX   VI   UT   VT   VA   ?

250. Suppose you enter an elevator at a certain floor. Then the elevator moves up 5 floors, down 3 floors, and up 2 floors. If you are then at the 8th floor, on what floor did you first enter the elevator?

251. Five students in a third-grade class scored in the 90's on a math test. Use the information given below and complete the chart to find out each student's score. Mark an X in a space when it cannot be the answer. Mark an O to show the correct score.

	99	97	95	94	91
Mindy					
Tess					
Ben					
Hector					
Khalid					

1. The scores were 99, 97, 95, 94, and 91.

2. Mindy scored higher than Hector and Tess.

3. Tess scored 94.

4. Ben scored higher than most but not higher than everyone.

5. Mindy did not get the highest score.

Copyright © 2009 by John Wiley & Sons, Inc.

Copyright © 2009 by John Wiley & Sons, Inc.

252. If Kelsey's daughter is my daughter's mother, what am I to Kelsey?

    a. Grandmother

    b. Mother

    c. Daughter

    d. Granddaughter

    e. I am Kelsey.

    f. There's no way to know.

253. Take a good look at the capital letters below. Pay close attention to how they are constructed.

            A   H   K   N   W

One of the following letters belongs with the five capital letters—based on a characteristic of the way the letter is built. Can you tell me which letter belongs with the group and why?

    a. E

    b. L

    c. X

    d. Z

Just for Fun: Frame Game

254. Find the hidden word or phrase.

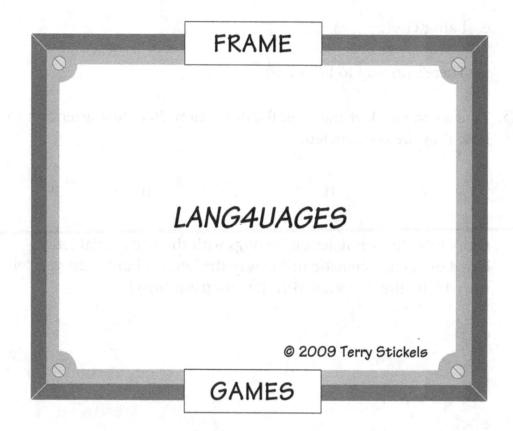

FRAME

LANG4UAGES

© 2009 Terry Stickels

GAMES

255. Each word in parentheses below was formed from the two words on either side of it. The same method was used in all four examples.

SNIP (NICE) PACE

TEAR (EAST) FAST

TRAY (RARE) FIRE

POUT (OURS) CARS

Based on the way the words in parentheses were created above, what word belongs in the parentheses below?

CANE (?) BATS

256. Doug and Marcia had taken their little sister Donna to the petting zoo. On the way home, Donna remarked, "I wish I were taller. About all I could see were the legs of the goats and the attendants. I did count 30 legs total of both humans and goats."

Doug replied, "That's interesting because I think there were the same number of goats as attendants at the petting zoo."

How many of each were at the petting zoo?

Copyright © 2009 by John Wiley & Sons, Inc.

257. An analogy is a kind of word puzzle. Figure out the relationship of the first two words in the puzzle. Then look for an answer in the second part of the puzzle that will keep the same relationship. Here's an example:

white : black : : day : ?

This reads: "White is to black as day is to ?." The answer, of course, is "night." Here's another example:

bicycle : 2 : : car : ?

This reads: "Bicycle is to two as car is to ?." A bicycle has two wheels, and a car has four wheels. Four is the correct answer.

Solve these coin and paper money analogies:

a. 1 : Washington : : ? : Lincoln

b. Nickel : Dime : : $.50 : ?

c. 1 : Lincoln : : 5 : ? (choose one: Truman, Jefferson, Harding)

d. $1 : $100 : : $10 : ?

Copyright © 2009 by John Wiley & Sons, Inc.

258. Take three Kings and three Queens from a normal deck of playing cards. The goal is to be able to place these six cards in alternating order—King, Queen, King, Queen, King, Queen—following a specific set of rules. Here are the rules:

1. Start with all the six cards in your hand, face down.

2. Take the top card and place it on the bottom of the cards in your hand.

3. Place the second card face up on the table. This should be your first King.

4. Place the next card (the third card) on the bottom of the cards in your hand.

5. Take the next card and place it face up on the table.

6. Continue alternating the cards like this until all six cards are face up on the table and in the order of: King, Queen, King, Queen, King, Queen.

Now here's the puzzle: In what order should the cards be arranged in your hand before you start so you can place them correctly on the table? Be careful—the answer may surprise you!

HINT
The second card has to be a King, and the fourth card has to be a Queen!

Copyright © 2009 by John Wiley & Sons, Inc.

259. Some of the most fun puzzles to solve are anagrams—words having letters that can be arranged into new words. Here are two examples: "race" also can be "care," and "dare" can be rearranged into "read." Sometimes words have more than one anagram. The word "trace" can be "react," "cater," "crate," and "caret."

Math words make great anagrams. The letters in "triangles" can make the two-word phrases "real sting" and "sing later." "Rectangles" might be "gentle arcs" or "regal scent." In the left-hand column below are math words to be matched with their respective anagrams in the right-hand column.

a.	fractions	he owns lumber
b.	decimal point	a metric hit
c.	acute angles	so frantic
d.	whole numbers	mild canoe tip
e.	arithmetic	a clean guest

Copyright © 2009 by John Wiley & Sons, Inc.

260. Braille is a coded system used by blind people to read and write. It was devised in 1821 by Louis Braille. Each character, or "cell," is arranged in a 3 × 2 rectangle where combinations of the six "dots" are filled in to make the letters. The dots are raised so they can be felt easily with the fingertips. Braille is read from left to right. Below is the alphabet in Braille.

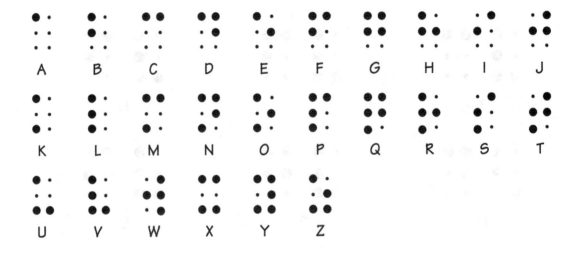

a. What would be the maximum number of characters you could make using any or all of the six dots?

b. Even if the dots are not raised, Braille can be used to create fun coded messages. What letter, in Braille, is missing from the sequence below?

 ?

Copyright © 2009 by John Wiley & Sons, Inc.

261. The number system in Braille is based on the same system, but it is expanded into multiple six-cell units. Here are some examples.

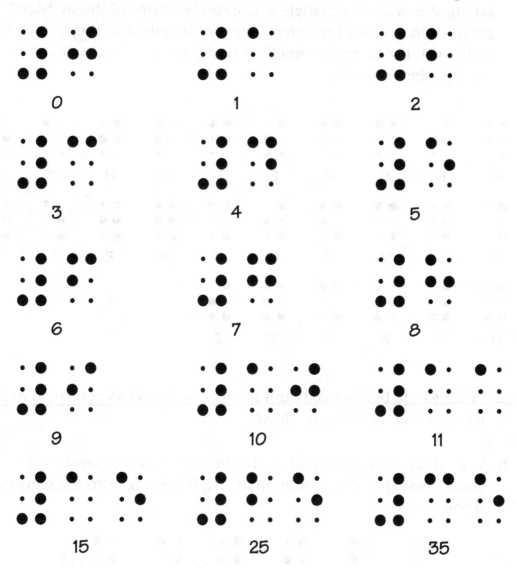

Copyright © 2009 by John Wiley & Sons, Inc.

After looking at the chart, you can see how the pattern develops and you can create any number you wish. The first six-dot unit is always the same and lets you know that what follows is a number.

a. How would you write 50?

b. 100?

c. The year 2007?

d. What number (in Braille) goes where the question mark is in the fraction below?

$$\frac{\vcenter{\hbox{⠃ ⠊ ⠙}}}{?} = \frac{1}{2}$$

Copyright © 2009 by John Wiley & Sons, Inc.

262. Morse code originally was created to send telegraphic information over wires. Samuel Morse developed an electric telegraph around 1835, and it was used for many years by the railroads and armed services, as well as the general public. Today it is used primarily by amateur radio operators and for some military communications.

The system was developed to use standardized sequences of short and long units (called dots and dashes) to represent letters, numbers, symbols, and punctuation. The short and long messaging can be formed by sounds, marks, or electronic pulses. Here's a chart of what the code looks like written out:

A	.-	N	-.	1	.----	Ñ	--.--	N with tilde
B	-...	O	---	2	..---	Ö	---.	O with umlaut
C	-.-.	P	.--.	3	...--	Ü	..--	U with umlaut
D	-..	Q	--.-	4	....-	,	--..--	comma
E	.	R	.-.	5	.....	.	.-.-.-	period
F	..-.	S	...	6	-....	?	..--..	question mark
G	--.	T	-	7	--...	;	-.-.-.	semicolon
H	....	U	..-	8	---..	:	---...	colon
I	..	V	...-	9	----.	/	-..-.	slash
J	.---	W	.--	0	-----	–	-....-	dash
K	-.-	X	-..-	Á	.--.- A with accent	'	.----.	apostrophe
L	.-..	Y	-.--	Ä	.-.- A with umlaut	( )	-.--.-	parenthesis
M	--	Z	--..	É	..-.. E with accent	_	..--.-	underline

Copyright © 2009 by John Wiley & Sons, Inc.

a. The number 1233 is below. What is represented by the shaded section?

b. How would you write $\dfrac{1}{2}$?

c. What does the following sentence say?

d. You can have fun with all types of codes because you can create your own symbols and characters. What numbers (in Morse code) belong in the denominations of the fractions below? Notice that I used both the "slash" symbol (/) and the = sign, both symbols found in math but represented by dots and dashes in Morse code.

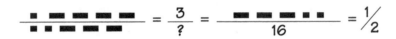

Copyright © 2009 by John Wiley & Sons, Inc.

263. A father says to his friend, "That's one of my sons sitting over there." His friend asks the father, who is a mathematician, how many kids he has. The father replies, "My son has as many sisters as he has brothers. Each of his sisters has twice as many brothers as she has sisters." How many sons and daughters does the mathematician have?

Copyright © 2009 by John Wiley & Sons, Inc.

Just for Fun: Frame Game

264. Find the hidden word or phrase.

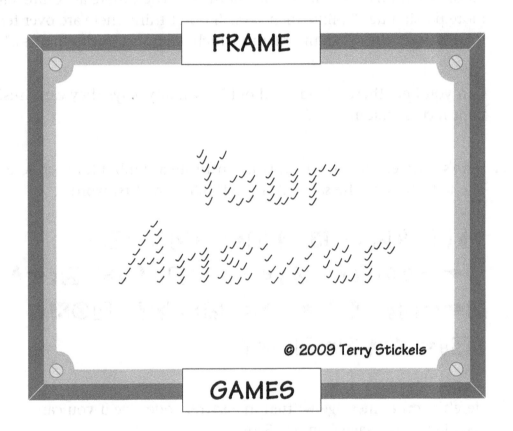

FRAME

Your Answer

© 2009 Terry Stickels

GAMES

265. If six people are in a room and each person shakes hands with everyone else one time, and one time only, how many total handshakes take place?

266. Millie, Molly, and Mookie are three friends who compete with each other in just about everything they do. They are going to race each other in a 50-yard sprint in a swimming pool. Molly says, "There are only six possibilities of our finishing order in this race." But Mookie reminds her, "Not if you count ties. Then there are quite a few more possibilities." Millie then says, "I don't think there are over ten total ways of the different order in which we finish, including ties."

Can you help these friends find out how many ways they can finish their race, including ties?

267. Here's a secret code in which you substitute a symbol for each letter. The letter Y stays the same. ALLIGATORS is the first word.

268. Here's another message written in a secret code. See if you can decode this message from Dr. Seuss:

ROFM ERTHE OT ERHE, NAD ERHE OT ERTHE,

NUFYN GNISTH RAE

RYHWREEVEE. —RD. ESUSS

Copyright © 2009 by John Wiley & Sons, Inc.

269. How would you punctuate the following sentence to make it true?

There are eight letters in this note.

270. Ms. Guard, Ms. Forward, and Ms. Center were having fun after practice one day. "Everyone is always getting us confused because none of us has the same name as the position we play," said Ms. Center. "I know," said the person who plays guard. "I think it's fun to see the looks on people's faces when we try to explain it to them." From this quick conversation, can you tell which person plays each position?

271. Joe, Larry, Lucy, and Brenda are 12, 11, 10, and 9, but not necessarily in that order. We do know that the consecutive ages alternate girl, boy, girl, boy . . . from oldest to youngest. These clues will help:

- Lucy is a year older than Joe.

- Joe is younger than Larry.

From these two clues, can you tell me the age of each person?

272. Five of the six phrases below are anagrams of Boston Celtics. Which phrase is incorrect?

    a. Bent Coil Costs   d. Best Icon-Colts

    b. Bisect On Clots   e. Colts Bite Once

    c. Sonic Cost Belt   f. Nicest Cob List

Copyright © 2009 by John Wiley & Sons, Inc.

273. A zookeeper is moving three snakes to a new area of the zoo. The three snakes don't always get along, so the zookeeper is always close by to make sure everything is okay. She has to be careful about which snakes are together when she isn't around. She has to figure out a way to transport them so there isn't a problem. She can't put the Anaconda with the Boa, and she can't leave the Boa with the King Cobra or transport them together. How can she move all three snakes and not worry about which snakes are left alone or which can be transported safely together? She has to move one at a time.

274. Martha and her father are driving on the Interstate at exactly 60 miles per hour. They're headed due east. They hear on the radio that a thunderstorm is directly behind them 100 miles and heading due east. There are no other storms in any direction. After 3 hours of driving, it started to rain on Martha's dad's car. What conclusion listed below is valid for certain?

a. The rain was not from the thunderstorm they heard about on the radio 3 hours ago.

b. The rain came from the north at exactly the same time they were driving that part of the highway.

c. The storm they heard about was moving faster than 60 miles per hour.

d. It wasn't really rain, but sleet.

Copyright © 2009 by John Wiley & Sons, Inc.

275. Each grouping of three words below shares a common trait seen in each word. The trait is different for each of the five different sets. Here's an example:

total   talking   fatality

Answer: Each word has "tal" in it.

Try these: What's the common trait in these word sets?

a.   localize   calendar   practical

b.   entertainment   hotshot   restores

c.   magazine   delivery   education

d.   defy   first   study

e.   outlook   corporation   doorknob

276. Reggie left home one summer evening with gloves and protective headgear. Actually, he left home in a dead sprint. After a short distance, he stopped. He caught his breath and then did something that surprised the people watching him: He stole something. After a few minutes, he took off in a dead sprint again. This time he wasn't going to stop until he got home. When he finally got into a position where he could see home clearly, he knew there was going to be trouble. There, as plain as day, was a man who was going to block his arrival. The man meant business. He wasn't going to let Reggie by him, no matter what. Reggie was bound and determined to get by him even if there was a terrible collision—which there was. What had just taken place?

277. Can you think of a situation where the faster an object travels, the longer it will take to reach its destination?

Copyright © 2009 by John Wiley & Sons, Inc.

Just for Fun: Frame Game

278. Find the hidden word or phrase.

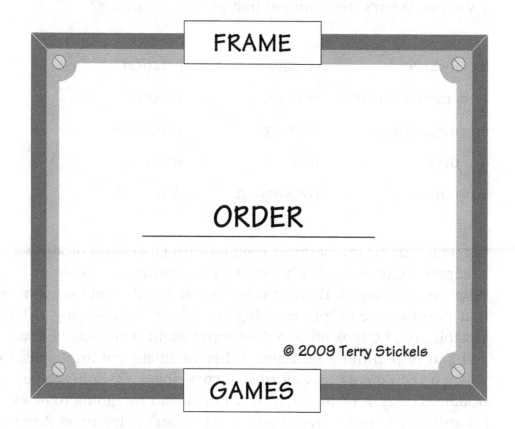

FRAME

ORDER

GAMES

© 2009 Terry Stickels

Copyright © 2009 by John Wiley & Sons, Inc.

279. Claudia Marcos was 32 years old in 1723, but in 1718 she was 37. How is this possible?

280. Rachel's school is having "reverse day," where things that normally are done are now done backward. For example, the school is having a dinner in the morning, instead of breakfast. The last class of a normal school day is now the first class. The math teacher is having a bike race—but with a twist. The bicycle that finishes last wins a prize. The teacher assigns each bike at random to the students so no one has an advantage. The problem is that the race can last only 30 minutes because of other classes, so the race has to move quickly. The teacher has an ingenious idea of how to make this work. What did he suggest?

281.

We know that tomorrow

Follows today

That's true on land

And seas, I say

But there's one place

And it's not new

Where yesterday's after

Today—it's true!

Where is this true?

282. Two horses are in a field. One is facing due west and the other is facing due east. They can see each other without turning around. How can they do this?

283. In an old puzzle a person is driving down the highway at the legal speed limit. He is sober, has proper plates and insurance, and is wearing a seatbelt. He apparently is doing everything correctly, but a patrolman pulls him over and gives him a ticket. Why? Because he was driving in the wrong direction. All the other cars were going in the opposite direction on that side of the highway.

Now here's the new puzzle:

The same set of circumstances leading up to the arrest: proper speed, plates, insurance, seatbelt. No drinking, no tail lights missing, or any careless driving. This time the man was driving down the correct side of the highway—and was arrested for a serious infraction. What could he possibly have done incorrectly?

284. The professor was found dead with his calculator next to him in the library. The time of death was well after midnight. His body was lying facing a large mirror. His calculator had the number 11345 on it. This wasn't unusual, as he worked on equations all day. The professor had scheduled a series of half-hour appointments that day, but they were all with friends and family: Linda, Bill, Christy, Shelley, his brother, and Marty. No other people had access to the library. The detective immediately knew who the murderer was. How?

Copyright © 2009 by John Wiley & Sons, Inc.

285. Can you figure out what words are represented by the numbers below?

a. What four numbers mean a cry for assistance?

b. What six numbers represent the place you are Monday to Friday?

c. What five numbers is a lovable and furry baby animal that likes to lick you?

286. What do you call a knight caught in a windstorm?

2   5 7 1 4 6 7 5 1 2 3 8

The answer to the riddle is written in the code above. Use the clues below to help you determine the riddle's answer.

If A − 1 = 1, then A = ?   If T − H = A, then H = ?

If A + 3 = N, then N = ?   If H − 3 = G, then G = ?

If I − N = 2, then I = ?   If T + A = E, then E = ?

If T − A = 4, then T = ?   If N − H + A = L, then L = ?

Copyright © 2009 by John Wiley & Sons, Inc.

287. Two-Brain Howie (as he is affectionately known because he is so smart) is walking in Logicland when he comes to a street sign that looks like this:

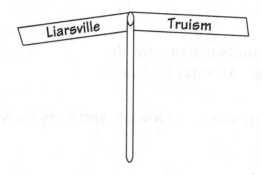

Howie knows that Liarsville is a town where everyone lies all the time. Truism, of course, is a town of people who speak nothing but the truth. Then, from behind a tree, a boy walks toward Howie and asks, "How may I help you?" Howie says, "I don't know if that sign is accurate. It may have been placed there by a citizen of Liarsville." The boy responds, "Hmm. That's a good point. But there's one question you can ask me that will assure you the correct information. Do you know what that question is?" Howie doesn't know if this boy is a liar or a truth-teller, so he has to be very careful. Can you help Howie out?

Copyright © 2009 by John Wiley & Sons, Inc.

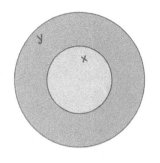

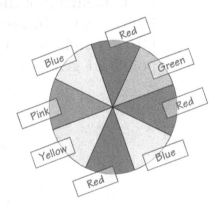

Part IV

ALGEBRA, STATISTICS, and PROBABILITY

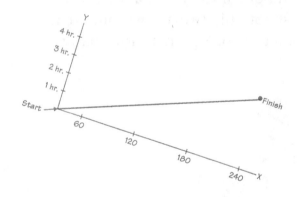

288. The U.S. swim team won 13 gold medals in a recent competition against two other countries. Of the total 60 medals awarded, there were 20 each of bronze, silver, and gold. Spain won 5 gold medals. France won one-third of all the medals and had an equal number of silver and bronze medals. How many silver and bronze medals did France win?

289. Penny and Brenda each shot four arrows at the target shown below. Penny shot two arrows into "x" and two into "y" for a score of 16. Brenda shot three into "x" and one into "y" for a total of 14. Molly stopped by but had time to shoot only two arrows; one went into "x" and one went into "y" for a total of 8 points. How many points are given for a shot into "x"?

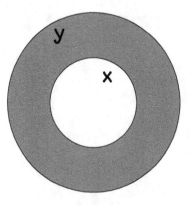

Copyright © 2009 by John Wiley & Sons, Inc.

Copyright © 2009 by John Wiley & Sons, Inc.

290. If $A + B = C + D$ and A and B are both whole positive numbers, then:

    a. C and D each have to be whole numbers.

    b. $A \times B = C \times D$

    c. Neither C nor D can be negative.

    d. Either C or D has to be positive, at the least.

    e. None of the above choices are correct.

291. Marla noticed that her friend Ron had three times as many pieces of candy as she did. She told him, "If you give me seven pieces of your candy, we'll have exactly the same number of pieces." Ron responded, "I didn't know that until you mentioned it. But I'll make you a deal: If you can show me how to solve this puzzle using algebra, I'll give you the seven pieces."

One minute later, Ron was shocked to see that Marla had solved it perfectly. Can you do the same?

292. Rene was reading a book and noticed that the sum of the last three pages she had just finished reading totaled 345. She mentioned this to her mom, who said, "I can tell you what those page numbers are if you give me a few seconds. I'm going to solve this by using 'x' to represent the first of the three page numbers." Can you help Rene's mom come up with the three page numbers?

Just for Fun: Frame Game

293. Find the hidden word or phrase.

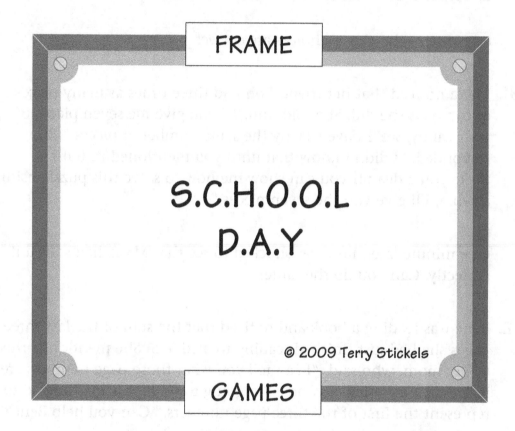

FRAME

S.C.H.O.O.L
D.A.Y

© 2009 Terry Stickels

GAMES

294. In the addition puzzle of
$$
\begin{array}{r}
AB \\
+AB \\
\hline
CA
\end{array}
$$

A, B, and C are all positive integers, each having a different value. What are the values of each of the letters? Do not consider the number 1 in this puzzle.

295. Here is a puzzle called a Number Cross.

$$
\begin{array}{ccc}
A & B & C \\
& & D \\
& & E \\
F & G & H \\
\end{array}
$$

Each of the eight letters is a different number from 1 to 8.
A + B + C = F + G + H = 12.   D + E = 12.   C + D + E + F = 26.
D = 5.   A, B, and C are even numbers. H = 1. What are the values of each letter?

296. Doug looked at his friend Roland and said, "I'm thinking of two numbers whose sum is 160, and one of the numbers is three times the other. I'll bet you can't show me a way to figure this out on paper. If you can, the ice cream is on me."

Roland grabbed a pencil and wrote down a way to do it, with "x" representing the smaller of the two numbers. He enjoyed a large chocolate shake, which tasted even better because he didn't have to buy it.

Could you have shown Doug how to do this—and had some ice cream, too? What are the two numbers?

Copyright © 2009 by John Wiley & Sons, Inc.

297. Tilly Sommers is the leading hitter for average on her softball team. She currently is hitting .425. That means if she were to have 1,000 plate appearances, she would hit safely 425 times. Her hits could be anything from a single to a home run. Tilly has been up to the plate 200 times this year. How many hits does she currently have?

298. Linda had an average of 93 on three math tests covering algebra. She also had an average of 96 on four tests covering geometry. She got an 89 on one math test covering land area. If all the tests had the same number of questions and were treated as equal parts of her math grade, what was her overall average?

HINT
Remember—it makes a difference as to how many tests each section contains.

299. Samantha complained to her dad, "I'm supposed to mix this solution together for a science experiment at school, but I don't have the right measuring device. All I have is this beaker that is marked in twelfths. The instructions call for $\frac{3}{7}$ of a beaker that is the same size as mine. I must have picked up the wrong beaker at school."

Her dad replied, "That still shouldn't be too difficult to accomplish. Even though it may not be perfectly exact, we can get the desired result. You just have to think about how to convert $\frac{3}{7}$ into twelfths."

How would you convert $\frac{3}{7}$ into twelfths?

300. Two sisters are running laps around the school track to raise money for the school tennis team. Regina had time to run only one lap on the first day, and her sister Rellie ran six laps. They both agreed to run one lap a day each day after their first day's run. How many days will it be before Rellie has run twice as far as Regina?

Copyright © 2009 by John Wiley & Sons, Inc.

301. Below is a graph that Maria's father drew of a trip they took in the car. Her father drove at the same speed for the entire trip and didn't stop.

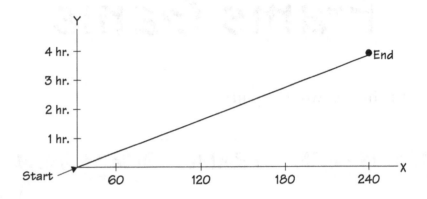

On the vertical line known as the Y-axis, the time that the trip took is marked hour by hour. On the horizontal line known as the X-axis, the miles of the trip are marked in units of 60 miles at a time.

a. How long did the trip take?

b. How far did they go?

c. Can you tell anything about the speed at which Maria's father drove?

302. Margaret's uncle has two children. One of them is a boy. What are the chances that her uncle has one girl and one boy?

303. A man knew he had 26 socks in his top drawer. There were 6 blue socks, 8 brown socks, and 12 black socks. He wasn't tall enough to see which color socks he needed, so he had to grab the loose socks at random.

What is the least number of socks the man would have to pull to make certain that he had a pair of blue socks?

Copyright © 2009 by John Wiley & Sons, Inc.

Just for Fun: Frame Game

304. Find the hidden word or phrase.

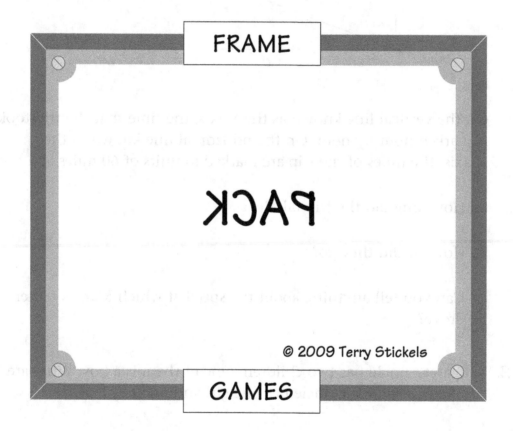

FRAME

PACK

© 2009 Terry Stickels

GAMES

305. A spinner wheel is divided into 8 sections: 3 sections are red, 2 are blue, 1 is pink, 1 is yellow, and 1 is green.

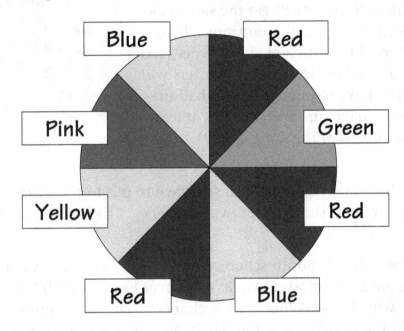

a. If you spin the spinner once, what is the probability that you will land on blue?

b. If you start again and spin the spinner once, what are the chances the spinner will *not* land on red?

c. What are the chances that you will land on red or green?

d. If you spin the spinner, what are the chances of landing on blue divided by the chances of landing on red?

Copyright © 2009 by John Wiley & Sons, Inc.

306. Dinesha is babysitting her two younger brothers, who want gum from a gumball machine. If they don't get the same color gumball, they'll have a tantrum. There are three different colored gumballs—red, blue, and white. How many quarters will Dinesha have to put in the gumball machine to make sure that she gets at least two gumballs of the same color?

HINT
Think of all the possibilities. Remember—you have to know for certain.

Now, how many quarters will she have to put in the machine to make sure that she and her two brothers get the same color gumball?

307. For the entire 9-month school year, Jamie's mom makes either cookies or pie 2 days a week. Jamie just never knows which 2 days his mom will choose. What are the chances that Jamie's mom will make one of the desserts on a Tuesday in March? For the purposes of this puzzle, consider each month to have 4 weeks. The school year runs from September to May. What if you based your answer on the entire 12 months?

Copyright © 2009 by John Wiley & Sons, Inc.

Answers
Part I. Numbers and Operations

Whole Numbers

1. The answer is 49. The difference between each two consecutive numbers grows in the order of 3, 5, 7, 9, 11, and 13—all odd numbers. (*Note:* These numbers also are called "consecutive square numbers" because they are all of the square numbers in a row: $1^2 = 1$, $2^2 = 4$, $3^2 = 9$, $4^2 = 16$, etc. So what is the number after 49? 64.

2.

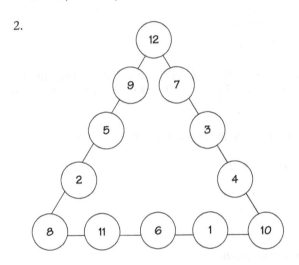

3. a. He will make 5×5 hours, or $25.00 each day he works. Since he works 5 days a week, he will make 25×5, or $125.00 per week.

   b. He works 5 weeks total at $125.00 per week, so he will make $125 \times 5 = $625.00 for the entire 5 weeks.

4. They ended up spending $120 dollars in total.

Brenda paid	– $75.00	Brenda's mom paid – $60.00
Brenda sold glove	+ $65.00	
Brenda bought old glove	– $50.00	
	– $125.00	– $60.00
	+ $65.00	
	– $60.00	
TOTAL:		–$60 + –$60 = –$120.00

5. ◁ = 10

Answers to exercises:
a. 19
b. 100
c. 91
d. 91
e. 91
f. 89
g. 38
h. 101
i. 909
j. 101

6. Mrs. Johnson paid $225 total for the iPod. A 10% discount would result in a reduction of $\frac{1}{10}$ of the price, or $25.

$$\begin{array}{r} \$250.00 \\ -\$25.00 \\ \hline \$225.00 \end{array}$$

7. Since a 1 is carried to B + C, making their total 16, B + C must equal 15. The only two digits that can total 15 are <u>8</u> and <u>7</u>. (We don't know which letter is which value, but the problem didn't ask for this.)

8. The missing number is 6. The two numbers opposite each other always total 21:

$$15 + 6 = 21$$

The other numbers:

$$17 + 4 = 21$$
$$13 + 8 = 21$$
$$11 + 10 = 21$$

9. The missing number is 3. The logic of the puzzle is:

$$6 \times 3 = 1\underline{8}$$
$$4 \times 9 = 3\underline{6}$$
$$7 \times 5 = 3\underline{5}$$
$$9 \times 3 = 2\underline{7}$$
$$3 \times 8 = 2\underline{4}$$

10. The missing number is 24. The rule is to double the first number in each rectangle and place that number in the next box below it.

11. The missing number is 4. The sum of the three numbers in each box is 12.

12. The letter A is a 6 and the letter B is 5. A little experimentation will reveal that 5, added three times, is the only number, besides zero, that will have the same number as the three numbers that were added. If the 1 were not carried to the A column, you can see that three A's would equal 18. So each A must equal 6.

13.
```
        F = 1
  928   O = 8
 +928   R = 6
 1856   T = 9
        U = 5
        W = 2
```

14. Yearly Checkup

15. a. The answer is 100. $4 \times 4 = 16 :: 10 \times 10 = 100$

    b. Octagon → A triangle has 3 sides; a hexagon has 6 sides. So it is a ratio of 3 to 6, which is the same as 1 to 2. A rectangle has 4 sides; an octagon has 8 sides. So it is a ratio of 4 to 8, which is the same as 1 to 2.

16. The missing number is 3. The sum of the bottom two numbers in each circle is one-half the number at the top of the circle.

17. a. 59 = LIX   e. LXIX = 69

    b. 88 = LXXXVIII   f. MCD = 1400

    c. 449 = CDXLIX   g. 2,919 = MMCMXIX

    d. MXLVII = 1,047   h. CMXCIX = 999

18. She made four 2-point shots and three 3-point shots.

$$
\begin{array}{r}
4 \times 2 = 8 \\
3 \times 3 = 9 \\
\hline
17 \text{ Points}
\end{array}
$$

This is a great puzzle for experimenting. You know that Joan's sister made an even number of 2-point shots. So try two 2-point shots worth 4 points: $17 - 4 = 11$. This can't be right because 11 is not evenly divisible by 3. Try four 2-point shots worth 8 points. And this works: $17 - 8 = 9$ points, which is three 3-point shots. See what happens with six 2-point shots and eight 2-point shots. You'll see that four 2-point shots is the only answer that fits!

19. Here are some different ways to arrive at 100 using the numbers 1 through 9:

$$12 + 34 + 5 \times 6 + 7 + 8 + 9 = 100$$

$$12 + 3 + 4 - 56 \div 7 + 89 = 100$$

20. Problem c. is the same as 7.

$$10 - 4 = 6 + \frac{1}{1} = 6 + 1 = 7$$

21.

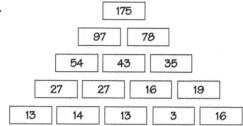

22. 8.42

23. B is 8. The only possibility is 8 + 7 = 15, where the 1 is carried over to represent D.

24. Here's one way to solve this. Each side totals 9.

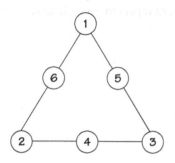

Are there more solutions?

25.

			4						
0	+	0	+	5	=	5			
			1					8	
			=					+	
		1	5	+	0	=	7	+	8
1			+				–		=
–			6				3		1
0	+	1	0	=	9	+	1		6
=		0	7				7		
3		–					–		
–		2			9	–	3	=	1	5	–	9
2		=							
		9							
		–							
		1							

26. The third fifth-grader's shoe size was $6\frac{3}{4}$. The fourth-graders' shoe sizes added up to

$$20\frac{1}{2} \rightarrow 6\frac{1}{3} + 8\frac{1}{2} + 5\frac{2}{3} = 20\frac{1}{2}$$

The two fifth-graders' shoe sizes were $7\frac{1}{4} + 6\frac{1}{2} = 13\frac{3}{4}$. Subtract this from $20\frac{1}{2}$ to get the third fifth-grader's shoe size:

$$
\begin{array}{r}
20\frac{1}{2} \\
-13\frac{3}{4} \\
\hline
6\frac{3}{4}
\end{array}
$$

27. The answer is 41.

   $[(4 + 2) + (4 \times 2)] + [(3 + 6) + (3 \times 6)] = (6 + 8) + (9 + 18) = 14 + 27 = 41$

28. The answer is b. Loafers would cost $3.00. The shoes' prices were based on the number of vowels in the spelling of each type of shoe → $1.00 per vowel.

29. A 5 goes back to circle #1 and an 8 goes back to circle #2. An easy way to solve this is to realize that since the circles have the same sum, all the numbers added together are equal to twice the numbers in each circle. So $9 + 13 + 6 = 28$ and $\frac{1}{2}$ of 28 is 14. For its numbers to add up to 14, circle 1 needs a 5 ($9 + 5 = 14$) and circle 2 needs an 8 ($8 + 6 = 14$).

30. Again, first add all the numbers → $14 + 9 + 10 + 39 = 72$.

   Since there are *three* circles, you divide the total by 3 to find that each circle has numbers that total 24 ($72 \div 3 = 24$). So circle #1 is $14 + 10$; circle #2 is $9 + 15$; and circle #3 is $10 + 14$.

31. a. The missing number is 19. You find the number by adding the numbers on top of each other in the box on the left.

   b. The missing number is 0. You find the number by subtracting the bottom number from the top number in the box on the left.

   c. The missing number is 7. You find the number by dividing the bottom number by the top number directly above it.

   d. The missing number is 100. You find the number by multiplying the top number by the bottom number directly underneath it.

32. d. Two digits would have to be changed: the 1 and the 9. The 1 can be changed to a 9, and the 9 in 69 can be changed to a 4.

$$
\begin{array}{r}
96 \\
+64 \\
\hline
160
\end{array}
$$

There's another way to make the addition equal 160. Turn the addition problem upside down.

33. The missing number is 18. If you add the four numbers in the corners of each box, the sum will be the number in the middle box.

34. The next number is 7777777: 1 one, 2 twos, 3 threes, 4 fours, 5 fives, 6 sixes, and 7 sevens.

35. a. The number is 5. It is between 3 and 7, and the two numbers that total 10 are 4 and 6.

    b. The number is 12. It is less than 15 and greater than 9, and it's the middle number between 9 and 15.

    $$9, 10, 11, \underline{\mathbf{12}}, 13, 14, 15$$

    c. The number is 6. $(5 \times 2) + 3 + 7 - 6 = 14$

    14 divided by 7 is 2.

    2 times 3 is 6.

36. A = 3

    B = 1

    C = 4

    D = 9

    E = 6

37.

4	×	3	−	9	+	8	11
+	■	+	■	+	■	+	
8	×	9	+	3	−	4	71
+	■	×	■	+	■	−	
9	×	4	+	4	+	1	41
×	■	−	■	×	■	+	
3	+	8	−	2	+	9	18

39   31   20   20

38. Here are three answers. How many can you find?

283	283	283
540	140	170
+176	+576	+546
999	999	999

39.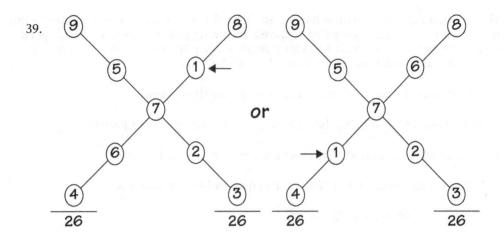

40. Seven students are not taking a language. Add 7 + 10 + 4 to get 21. Then subtract 21 from the total students: 28 – 21 = 7.

41. They sold 4 boxes of each kind. Since one box holds 12 and the other box holds 5 and you know they sold an equal number of each, you can think about this puzzle as if they sold 17 pears at a time. Since 68 ÷ 17 is 4, they sold 4 boxes of each.

42. Coloring Between the Lines

43. The number 50 will appear under A. Notice that all the numbers under G are the consecutive multiples of 7 starting with 7. That means 49 will be under G and 50 will be under A. Likewise, 14 × 7 = 98, so 98 will be under G and 100 will appear two more spaces after G, or back to B.

44. The person lived for 70 years. Think of the time as if it were on a number line.

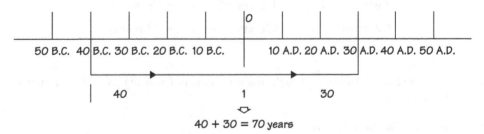

45. a. $(2 + 6) \times 4 = 32$

b. $(4 + 1) \times (5 + 5) = 50$

c. $(2 \times 3 \times 4) \div 6 = 4$

d. $(1 + 2 + 3) \div 6 = 1$

46. | 25 | 27 | 23 |

The first column increases by 3 from top to bottom. The second column increases by 4 from top to bottom. And the third column increases by 1, then 2, then 3, then 4 . . . so the last number should increase by 5 (18 + 5 = 23).

47. The first number that is divisible by 3, 4, and 5 is 60. One way to look at a puzzle like this is to multiply the numbers together to have a beginning point: $3 \times 4 \times 5 = 60$. A quick look at the factors of 60 shows no other number smaller. So any multiple of 60 (going higher) would also fit these parameters: 120, 180, 240, 300 . . .

48. a. The odd number out is 36. The other numbers are all multiples of 7.

    b. The odd number out is 26. The digits in the other numbers add up to 9.

    c. The odd number out is 45. The other numbers are all multiples of 8.

49. a. 8. The number to the left of 37 is 13. The number beneath that is 8.

    b. The three numbers are 9, 25, and 66.

    c. The last row. The sum of the six diagonal numbers is 178. The sum of the three numbers in the last row is 158:

    $$\begin{array}{r} 178 \\ -158 \\ \hline 20 \end{array}$$

50. The first friend had seven successful tosses and three that failed.

    The second friend had six successful tosses and four that failed.

    You can make a quick chart to show you the possible scores:

10 winners	0 losers	= 50 points
9 winners	1 loser	= 42 points
8 winners	2 losers	= 34 points
7 winners	3 losers	= 26 points
6 winners	4 losers	= 18 points

51. The number is 10. The sum of each row increases by 1 starting with the number 10 at the top.

52. a. $(8 + 7) \times 6 \div (6 - 1) = 18$

    b. $5 - 4 + 3 \times 2 \div 1 = 7$

53. The missing number is 14. Multiply the digits of each number together, beginning with the first number in each row, to determine the next number in the row.

54. All three will arrive every 12 days. That's because the least common multiplier for 2, 3, and 4 is 12. Since all three arrive every 12 days, you divide 365 by 12 and find that there are 30 times each year where all three will arrive on the same day.

55.

a.

9	–	1	–	6	= 2
+	■	×	■	+	
2	×	7	×	4	= 56
×	■	×	■	×	
5	×	8	+	3	= 43
=		=		=	
19		56		18	

b.

7	+	9	–	4	= 12
+	■	+	■	–	
2	+	6	–	1	= 7
×	■	×	■	+	
8	+	3	+	5	= 16
=		=		=	
23		27		8	

c.

1	×	8	×	3	= 24
×	■	–	■	×	
9	–	2	+	6	= 13
×	■	×	■	×	
7	×	5	+	4	= 39
=		=		=	
63		2		72	

d.

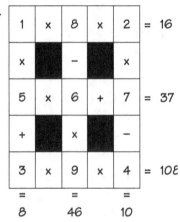

1	×	8	×	2	= 16
×	■	–	■	×	
5	×	6	+	7	= 37
+	■	×	■	–	
3	×	9	×	4	= 108
=		=		=	
8		46		10	

56. a. The second number is 9: 9 + 5 = 14 and 9 × 5 = 45

b. One of the numbers is 5, and the other number is 3: 5 + 3 = 8 and 5 × 3 = 15

c. One of the numbers is 9, and the other number is 4: 9 + 4 = 13 and 9 × 4 = 36

d. One of the numbers is 8, and the other number is 1: 8 + 1 = 9 and 8 × 1 = 8

57. Look Both Ways Before You Cross

58. According to the Game Ladder, Oklahoma would win by 22 points. Oklahoma beat Northwestern by 14; Northwestern beat Iowa by 1; and Iowa beat UCLA by 7. So 14 + 1 + 7 = 22 points.

59. The missing number is 12. When you look at the relationship of each set of top and bottom numbers, you'll see that 12 is 2 × 6, 24 is 3 × 8, 36 is 4 × 9, 45 is 5 × 9, 60 is 6 × 10, and 84 is 7 × 12.

60.   6 1 10 8
       5 9 2
         4 7
          3

61. The numbers on the left side of the line are all multiples of 6, and the numbers on the right side of the line are all multiples of 7.

   a. 98 is a multiple of 7, so it would fit on the right side of the line.

   b. 18 is a multiple of 6, so it would fit on the left side of the line.

   c. 42 would fit on either side because it is 6×7. 84 also would fit on either side.

62. Bess weighs 50 pounds, and Brandon weighs 70 pounds.

63.   947
    +42731
     43678

       A = 3
       C = 4
       E = 7
       I = 9
       K = 6
       M = 1
       R = 2
       S = 8

64.   2986
     +86
    3072

       A = 7
       E = 0
       H = 9
       I = 8
       N = 3
       S = 6
       T = 2

65. There are 25 boys and 15 girls. See the chart below.

5	10	15	20	25	30	35
to	to	to	to	to	to	to
3	6	9	12	15	18	21
↓	↓	↓	↓	↓	↓	↓
8	16	24	32	40	48	56
(5+3)	(10+6)	(15+9)	(20+12)	(25+15)	(30+18)	(35+21)

66. 150 miles. ADD the distance of 270 miles (Albion to Clarion) to the distance from Bloomfield to Deer Park, which is 350 miles: 270 + 350 = 620 miles. Now, SUBTRACT the 470 miles total distance from the 620: 620 − 470 = 150 miles.

67. The numbers were assigned starting with A = 1, B = 2, and counting in order until Z = 26. So:

B + E + E = 2 + 5 + 5 = 12

G + A + M + E = 7 + 1 + 13 + 5 = 26

Z + O + O = 26 + 15 + 15 = 56

S + C + H + O + O + L = 19 + 3 + 8 + 15 + 15 + 12 = 72

D + O + G = 4 + 15 + 7 = 26

I + S + L + A + N + D = 9 + 19 + 12 + 1 + 14 + 4 = 59

68. The correct answer should have been a. 3. You can work backward to find the answer. The number multiplied by 5 that has a result of 75 has to be 15. If 15 should have been divided by 5, then 3 would be the correct answer.

69. a. The missing number is 9. Add the top numbers and divide by 2 to get the bottom number:

$$32 + 20 = 52 \div 2 = 26$$

$$12 + 18 = 30 \div 2 = 15$$

$$8 + 10 = 18 \div 2 = \underline{9}$$

b. The missing number is 21. Multiply the top numbers and divide by 3 to get the bottom number:

$$8 \times 9 = 72 \div 3 = 24$$

$$3 \times 12 = 36 \div 3 = 12$$

$$9 \times 7 = 63 \div 3 = \underline{21}$$

70. The amounts they had left were: 20 cents, 25 cents, 30 cents, 35 cents, and 40 cents. Each of the friends could have only dimes and nickels, since no one had quarters or pennies. How many ways are there to combine four coins that are dimes and nickels?

   1. 4 dimes (40 cents)

   2. 3 dimes and 1 nickel (35 cents)

   3. 2 dimes and 2 nickels (30 cents)

   4. 1 dime and 3 nickels (25 cents)

   5. 4 nickels (20 cents)

71. a. The next number is 32. If the next shape is filled, then double the number. If the next shape is an outline, then subtract 4.

   b. The next number is 14. If the next shape is a four-sided shape, then subtract 4. If the next shape is not a four-sided shape, then add the number of sides.

   c. The next number is 25. Add 2 for each arrow.

72. Think Before You Act

73. Here are two—and there are more:

   a. 28 + 51 + 12 + 9

   b. 28 + 18 + 51 + 3

   The number 28 always must be in any grouping. Every other number is divisible by 3, so there is no way that 100 could ever be reached by using those numbers only, since 3 is not a factor of 100.

74.
$$5 \times 5 \text{ soldiers} \rightarrow 25 \text{ soldiers}$$
$$2 \text{ gold pips on 25 soldiers} \rightarrow 50 \text{ pips}$$
$$25 \text{ swords with brass tips} \rightarrow 25 \text{ swords}$$
$$25 \text{ soldiers} - 2 \text{ gloves each} \rightarrow 50 \text{ gloves}$$
$$25 \text{ soldiers} - \text{a star on each glove} \rightarrow 50 \text{ stars}$$
$$\underline{50 \text{ stars} \times 5 \text{ points} \rightarrow 250 \text{ points}}$$
$$450$$

(if you add the 25 brass tips, 475)

75. The missing number is 140. Look at the first four numbers. The diagonal numbers are the key. 6 is 2 times 3; 15 is 3 times 5. In the second grid, the diagonal numbers have a relationship of 3 times one number and 4 times one number. In the third grid, it's 4 and 5, in the fourth it's 5 and 6. So in the final grid, you multiply the 12 times 6 to get the 72 and the 20 times 7 to get 140. Here are two possible grids that would continue the sequence:

3	72
9	21

8	16
2	56

76.

9	6	2	1
15	12	8	7
21	18	14	13
27	24	20	19
33	30	26	25

Going across, the numbers in each row decrease by 3, 4, and 1 respectively. Going down, the numbers increase by 6 each time.

77. Here are some possible solutions:

	5					8					8	
	2					5					2	
1 4 3 7 9					4 9 3 7 1					1 7 3 9 4		
	8					6					6	
	6					2					5	

78. The odd one out is 78. It is 39 × 2. The other numbers are all evenly divisible by 37.

79.

		432	486		
	24	18	27		
	4	6	3	9	
2	2	3	1	9	

80. Each of the three hits in D was worth 20 points. Maria knew the value of A, B, and C, and the total value. She added A, B, and C, subtracted that total from 156, and then divided by 3.

Layer A = 6 hits → 6 points

Layer B = 8 hits → 40 points

Layer C = 5 hits → 50 points

96 points

There were 156 points total: 156 − 96 = 60, and 60 ÷ 3 = 20

81. a. 72 goes in the middle with 24 and 48

b. 40 goes in B

c. 36 goes in A

d. 25 doesn't go in either

e. 480 goes in the middle

82. Three possible factors of both 7 and 3 are: 21, 84, and 168.

Rational Numbers

83. My sister gave me 20 pennies and 20 nickels. One way to look at this puzzle is that since a penny is 1 cent and a nickel is 5 cents, I can think in terms of 6 cents. Since they are matched up equally, I can divide the 6 cents by the total. $1.20 divided by .06 is 20.

84. The pencil cost $.50. If the protractor was $2.00 more than the pencil, the protractor was $2.50 and the pencil was $.50.

85. Did I catch you? 72 divided by $\frac{1}{2}$ is 144. When dividing by a fraction, the rule is to invert and multiply.

$$72 \div \frac{1}{2} = 72 \times 2, \text{ or } 144$$

86. Brady runs for 85 minutes, or 1 hour, 25 minutes.

1 hour = 60 minutes

$\frac{3}{4}$ hour = 45 minutes

$\frac{2}{3}$ hour = 40 minutes

85 minutes

87. There will be 43 students in the drama club.

$\frac{3}{10}$ of the students are in band: $\frac{3}{10} \times 100 = 30$

$\frac{1}{10}$ are in tennis: $\frac{1}{10} \times 100 = 10$

17 play basketball

So 30 + 10 + 17 = 57. That leaves 43 students of our 100 available for drama club.

88. a. 64

b. $\frac{1}{4}$

c. 555 . . .

d. 14

89. $\frac{1}{10} \quad \frac{1}{5} \quad \frac{1}{3} \quad \frac{4}{9} \quad \frac{3}{5} \quad \frac{15}{17}$

90. $\frac{1}{16}$ or ♪. Here's another way to view this puzzle:

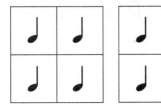

You can see that $\frac{1}{16} + \frac{1}{16} + \frac{1}{16} + \frac{1}{16} = \frac{1}{4}$ and that $\frac{1}{4} \times \frac{1}{4} = \frac{1}{16}$.

91. He put a decimal between the 8 and 9 to get 8.9.

92. He needs 8 containers of the $\frac{3}{4}$-cup milk boxes: $8 \times \frac{3}{4} = 6$

93. Jimmy grabbed $\frac{1}{3}$ of the pizza: $\frac{1}{3}$ of 12 is 4 pieces.

Mark took $\frac{1}{6}$ of the pizza: $\frac{1}{6}$ of 12 is 2 pieces.

Ernie took $\frac{1}{4}$: $\frac{1}{4}$ of 12 is 3 pieces.

Roberto also took $\frac{1}{6}$, or 2 pieces.

4 + 2 + 3 + 2 = 11 pieces of pizza were taken. That means only 1 piece was left.

94. a. $\dfrac{33}{3} = 11$

 b. $\dfrac{3}{3} + 3 = 4$

 c. $\dfrac{3}{(3+3)} = \dfrac{1}{2}$

 Did you find other ways?

95. d. 15. The lower number in each pair is a fraction of the upper number:

80		63		48		35		24		15	
8	$\dfrac{1}{10}$	7	$\dfrac{1}{9}$	6	$\dfrac{1}{8}$	5	$\dfrac{1}{7}$	4	$\dfrac{1}{6}$	3	$\dfrac{1}{5}$

96. Growing Restless

97. They are going to cut 30 trees, which is 3 times more than the 10 trees they cut in 1 day. They will need 3 times the days, or 3 days, to finish this project.

 It will take 1 day for the next project: 6 men can cut 10 trees in 1 day is the same as 12 men who cut 20 trees—and it takes the same time, 1 day: $\dfrac{6}{10} = \dfrac{3}{5}$ or $\dfrac{12}{20} = \dfrac{6}{10} = \dfrac{3}{5}$

98. c. 9. $\dfrac{3 \times 3 \times 3 \times 3}{3 + 3 + 3} = \dfrac{81}{9} = 9$

99. a. $\dfrac{15}{46}\left(\dfrac{15}{45} = \dfrac{1}{3}\right)$

100. The first thing is to see how many boxes of 2.5 pounds are in each 400-pound brick: $400 \div 2.5 = 160$ boxes. Since each box sells for $10.00, they can sell all 400 pounds for $160 \times \$10.00 = \$1,600.00$.

101. To make $.82, Allison has:

$$2 \text{ pennies} \rightarrow \$.02$$

$$2 \text{ nickels} \rightarrow \$.10$$

$$2 \text{ dimes} \rightarrow \$.20$$

$$\underline{2 \text{ quarters} \rightarrow \$.50}$$

$$\$.82$$

102. a. Dogs take up $\frac{5}{12}$ of the circle. $\frac{1}{9}+\frac{1}{12}+\frac{1}{6}+\frac{2}{9}=\frac{7}{12}$ of the circle, leaving $\frac{5}{12}$ of the circle to be for dog owners.

b. 75 kids. 180 total students $\times \frac{5}{12} = 75$

c. Bird owners are $\frac{1}{12}$ of the circle.

Dog owners are $\frac{5}{12}$ of the circle.

So the fraction of bird owners to dog owners is: $\dfrac{\frac{1}{12}}{\frac{5}{12}}=\frac{1}{5}$

d. $\frac{1}{2}$ the kids, or 90 students

$$\text{Fish} = \frac{2}{9}$$

$$\text{Cats} = \frac{1}{6}$$

$$\text{No Pets} = \frac{1}{9}$$

$$\frac{2}{9}+\frac{1}{6}+\frac{1}{9}=\frac{1}{3}+\frac{1}{6}=\frac{1}{2}$$

103. The total is $2.05. 5 pennies and 8 dimes are $.85. But there are 21 total coins, leaving 8 more coins. Since there are the same number of quarters and nickels, there must be 4 quarters and 4 nickels:

$$\begin{array}{r} 4 \text{ quarters} = \$1.00 \\ 4 \text{ nickels} = \$.20 \\ + \ \$.85 \\ \hline \$2.05 \end{array}$$

104. She had 10 dimes and 10 nickels. She gave $1.50 to the person who would be giving her change. Since the number of dimes and nickels are the same, you can look at the puzzle as a pairing of $.15—one dime and one nickel. $1.50 ÷ $.15 = 10 of each coin.

105. The third number would be $4\frac{7}{12}$. The first thing to note is that for three numbers to average 2, their total must be 3×2, or 6. You know the sum of two of the numbers: $\frac{2}{3}+\frac{3}{4}=\frac{8}{12}+\frac{9}{12}=\frac{17}{12}$ or $1\frac{5}{12}$. So to get the third number, you subtract $6-1\frac{5}{12}=4\frac{7}{12}$.

106. Prozillio would have 128 toenails! Make a chart to take a look at how numbers grow in puzzles like this.

Number of Cuts	Toenails
1	2
2	4
3	8
4	16
5	32
6	64
7	128

107. 15

108. The missing number is $\frac{1}{2}$. Starting with $\frac{1}{2}$ and looking at every other number, the sequence is $\frac{1}{2}$ $\frac{1}{3}$ $\frac{1}{4}$ $\frac{1}{5}$ $\frac{1}{6}$. Then, starting with $\frac{1}{6}$ and looking at every other number, you see the same sequence reversed: $\frac{1}{6}$ $\frac{1}{5}$ $\frac{1}{4}$ $\frac{1}{3}$ $\frac{1}{2}$.

109. The change adds up to $\frac{41}{100}$: $\$.01 + \$.05 + \$.10 + \$.25 = \$.41$

110. a. 60. The two lines are in a ratio of 5 to 3. So if line B reads 100, line A will read $\frac{3}{5}$ of 100, or 60.

    b. –40. $\frac{40}{24}$ has the same ratio as $\frac{20}{12} = \frac{10}{6} = \frac{5}{3}$

111. Walking Down the Stairs

112. Yes, you can: $99\frac{9}{9} = 100$, or $99 + \frac{9}{9} = 100$.

113. a. $\frac{2}{5} \times \frac{5}{8} = \frac{10}{40} = \frac{1}{4}$

    b. $\frac{3}{8} = .375$

    c. $44\% = \frac{44}{100} = \frac{22}{50} = \frac{11}{25}$

    d. $\frac{2}{9} = .2222\ldots$

$$9\overline{)20} \quad \begin{array}{r} .222 \\ \underline{18} \\ 20 \\ \underline{18} \\ 20 \\ \underline{18} \\ 2\ldots \end{array}$$

    e. $\frac{1}{3} + \frac{1}{2} = \frac{5}{6} = \frac{2}{6} + \frac{3}{6} = \frac{5}{6}$

    f. $4.4\% = .044$

114. The 18″ × 18″ pan will serve 32 people. Here's one way to look at this puzzle: Eight people eat 81 sq. in. of brownies ($9 \times 9 = 81$). 18″ × 18″ is 324 sq. in. of brownies. So, $\frac{81}{8}$ as $\frac{324}{?} = ? = 32$. The 18″ × 18″ will serve 4 times as many people, not twice as many!

115. 45 miles per hour. 3 miles in 4 minutes is the same as 45 miles in 60 minutes because

$$\frac{60 \text{ min}}{4 \text{ min}} = 15$$

$$15 \times 3 = 45 \qquad \frac{3 \text{ miles}}{4 \text{ minutes}} = \frac{45 \text{ miles}}{60 \text{ min}} \text{ or 1 hour}$$

116. a. (3) They are the same.

b. (1) $\dfrac{1}{2}+\dfrac{1}{7}=\dfrac{9}{14}$

$\dfrac{1}{3}+\dfrac{1}{6}=\dfrac{1}{2}$

$\dfrac{1}{4}+\dfrac{1}{5}=\dfrac{9}{20}$

117. a. 60 miles per hour. If something travels at 88 ft./sec., it would go 88×60 ft. in 1 minute. $88 \times 60 = 5,280$. So in 1 minute, it would travel 1 mile. In 1 hour, it would go 60 miles. So it traveled 60 mph.

b. 300 mph. One way to figure this out is to realize that 440 ft./sec. is 5 times 88 ft./sec. $60 \times 5 = 300$ mph.

118. a. She pushes the 50% button twice in a row.

b. She pushes the 200% button and then the 40% button.

c. $20\% \times 20\% \times 20\% = .8\%$, or $.008 = 8$ one-thousandths

119. b. $\dfrac{7}{8}$. The combinations of possibilities look like this:

Chocolate	Chocolate	Chocolate		Caramel	Caramel	Caramel
Chocolate	Chocolate	Caramel		Caramel	Caramel	Chocolate
Chocolate	Caramel	Caramel		Caramel	Chocolate	Chocolate
Chocolate	Caramel	Chocolate		Caramel	Chocolate	Caramel

In seven of the eight possibilities, there is at least one chocolate candy.

120. d. 76.384

121. Of the customers, 40 thought it was the third best-tasting candy and 280 thought it was the best-tasting candy. 48% of 1,000 is 480 people. That is the number of customers who liked *Chocolate Crunchers*. Of that group, one-third, or 160, thought it was the second best-tasting candy. And of 160, 25%, or $\dfrac{1}{4}$, thought it was the third best-tasting candy. $\dfrac{1}{4}$ of 160 is 40. So 40 people thought it was the third best-tasting candy. We know that 160 people thought it was the second best-tasting candy. Add that to the 40, and we have 200 people who thought it the second best or third best. 480 total people liked the candy—so $480 - 200 = 280$ people thought it was the best-tasting candy. (If you want to know what percentage that is, we find the percentage from the fraction $\dfrac{280}{480} = \dfrac{7}{12} = 58.333\%$.)

122. 72. $\dfrac{1}{2}$ of $\dfrac{1}{3}$ is $\dfrac{1}{6}$; $\dfrac{1}{6}$ of 36 is 6. $6 \times 6 = 36$. $36 \div \dfrac{1}{2} = 72$.

123. d. all of the above

Part II. Geometry and Measurement

Geometry

124. Pattern C cannot be folded into a cube.

125.

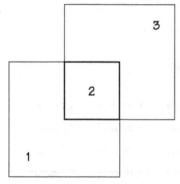

126. A 180° angle is a straight line: ————

127. 14 faces would be visible.

128. 12 sugar cubes

129. There are 16 of the smallest 1 × 1 size squares in the 4 × 4 grid.

There are 9 squares that are 2 × 2 in size.

There are 4 squares that are 3 × 3 in size.

And there is 1 large 4 × 4 square that consists of the four lines that make up the perimeter.

So there are 16 + 9 + 4 + 1 = 30 total squares of any size.

130. Illustration F does not belong. Each image has one fewer number of lines than the number of sides it has.

Triangle: 3 sides—2 lines

Square: 4 sides—3 lines

Pentagon: 5 sides—4 lines

Hexagon: 6 sides—5 lines

Octagon: 8 sides—should have 7 lines—but F has only 6 lines

131. Here's one solution.

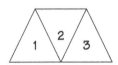

132.

133. There are 20 individual cubes.

134. There are five ways to fit four squares of the same size together.

135. Heptagon, which is a 7-sided figure.

The word after Nonagon is Decagon, which is a 10-sided figure.

Figure	Number of Sides
Triangle	3
Rectangle	4
Pentagon	5
Hexagon	6
Heptagon	7
Octagon	8
Nonagon	9
Decagon	10

Extra Credit: Dodecagon

136. 8:00 and 11:30 are times where the hands would form obtuse angles.

137. There are six different angles.

∠BAE   ∠CAE   ∠DAE
∠BAD   ∠CAD
∠BAC

138. a. Side A is 7 units long (notice the 3-unit and 4-unit section below A).

b. Side B is 10 units long (add A to the 3-unit section under the 6).

c. Side C is 3 units long (5 – 2).

139. Turn In Your Homework

140.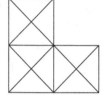

For two family members—any six triangles
For three family members—any four triangles
For four family members—any three triangles
For six family members—any two triangles

141. From above, the pyramid would look like illustration B.

142. 4 triangles. Here's one way to do this. See if you can find another.

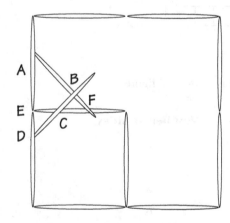

∇ABD
∇AEF
∇BCF
∇CDE

143. There are 6 × 2, or 12 faces glued together.

144. The missing letters are M, S, and J. They are oriented as shown below, with the M sideways.

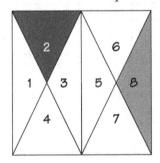

145. c. The perimeter of both rectangles together is always $1\frac{1}{2}$ times greater than the perimeter of the square.

146. D will not fold into a cube.

147. Polygon or quadrilateral

148. b. $\frac{1}{4}$. The square can be divided into eight sections having the same area, so two of those areas are equal to $\frac{1}{4}$ of the entire square.

149. You have 143 total sides.

$$7 \text{ triangles} = 7 \times 3 = 21$$

$$13 \text{ squares} = 13 \times 4 = 52$$

$$5 \text{ hexagons} = 6 \times 5 = 30$$

$$\underline{8 \text{ pentagons} = 8 \times 5 = 40}$$

$$143$$

150. c. 11

151. Lunch Break

152. View A is correct.

153. The 14″ square plus the 4″ square is equal to one of the sides of B. So B is a square with 18″ on each side. That means the rectangle has vertical sides of 33″ (18″ + 15″). It also means that the rectangle has horizontal sides of 32″. The bottom square between the 9″ square and the 15″ square is 8″ (9″ + 18″ + 15″ = 32″). That means A is 7″ because the 8″ square and A are equal to one of the sides of the 15″ square.

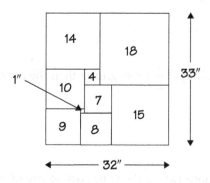

154.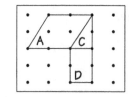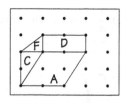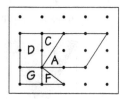

155. There are 11 cubes on the bottom layer. There are 2 cubes on the second layer and 1 on the top layer, for a total of 14 cubes.

156. The stack of cubes would look like diagram A.

157. In Figure A, you have a triangle   3 sides

              and a hexagon   <u>6 sides</u>

                                9 sides

    In Figure B, you have a square   4 sides

              and a pentagon   <u>5 sides</u>

                                  9 sides

    In Figure C, you have a pentagon   5 sides

       and it needs a 4-sided figure   <u>4 sides</u>

                                  9 sides

158. a. YZ is longer.

    b. They are equal in length.

    c. YZ is longer.

    d. AB is longer.

    e. AB is longer.

    f. They are equal.

Part II

Measurement

159. It will be Tuesday. Each week has 7 days, so it will be Thursday again in 21 days, and 2 days before that will be Tuesday.

160. d. 3. 45 days divided by 15 days is 3.

161. 204 inches. 5 yards is the same as 15 feet (3 feet = 1 yard). 15 feet + 2 feet = 17 feet. There are 12 inches in each foot. So 17 feet × 12 = 204 inches.

162. You slept 9 hours and 30 minutes. (2 hours and 45 minutes to midnight, plus 6 hours and 45 minutes = 9 hours and 30 minutes).

163. 11:00 AM. If 3 hours from now is 1:00 AM tomorrow, it must be 10:00 PM. And 11 hours before 10 PM is 11 AM. (10 hours earlier is noon, and 1 hour less is 11:00 AM.)

164. There are 324 inches in three Zoops. Three Zoops are the same as 9 yards. There are 3 feet in each yard, so there must be 9 × 3, or 27 feet in three Zoops. There are 12 inches in each foot, so there are 27 × 12 = 324 inches in three Zoops.

165. c. 6 days. The day after last Monday was Tuesday. If I came home 3 days before that, I came home on Saturday: Saturday, Sunday, Monday, Tuesday, Wednesday, and Thursday = 6 days.

166. The number of chimes totals 47.

167. There are $432 \frac{1}{16}$ -inch markings in 2 feet 3 inches. Each inch has 16 markings. There are 24 inches in 2 ft. Add 24 inches to 3 inches for a total of 27 inches. Then multiply $27 \times 16 = 432$ markings of $\frac{1}{16}$ inch.

168. Only one cube has only two sides painted gray. It's the middle cube.

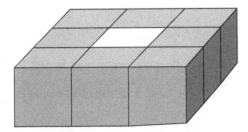

169. Box C should weigh 5 pounds. On the left side you have 5 ft. × 8 pounds, or 40 foot-pounds. We need 40 foot-pounds on the right side to make it balance. So 4 ft. × some number equals 40 ft.-lbs. We already have 5 lbs. So we must need 5 lbs. more to make it balance. 4 ft. × 10 lbs. = 40 ft.-lbs.

170. After 3 minutes and 37 seconds, you would have $2.17. 3 minutes = 180 seconds (60 seconds × 3). 180 + 37 seconds = 217 seconds. If you have a penny for every second, you have 217 cents, or $2.17.

After 4 hours and 13 minutes, you would have $151.80. 1 hour = 60 minutes × 60 seconds = 3,600 seconds. 4 hours = 3600 seconds × 4 = 14,400 seconds. 13 minutes = 60 seconds × 13 = 780 seconds. 14,400 seconds + 780 seconds = 15,180 seconds = 15,180 cents, or $151.80.

After one day, you would have $864. 1 day = 24 hours. 24 hours = 60 minutes × 24 hours = 1,440 minutes. 1,440 minutes × 60 seconds = 86,400 seconds. 86,400 seconds = 86,400 cents, or $864.00.

171. He filled the 4-liter container to the top and poured it into the 5-liter container. He then refilled the 4-liter container and poured 1 liter from it into the 5-liter container, which filled it. That left 3 liters in the 4-liter container.

172. The distance on each end is 3 inches. There are 7 letters in Melanie, but only 6 spaces between the letters. Each letter is 4 inches wide, so $7 \times 4 = 28$ inches taken up by the letters, plus 6 inches taken up by the spaces between the letters. $28 + 6 = 34$ inches. The banner is 40 inches, so there are 6 inches left over. Those 6 inches have to be cut in half for each side to be balanced. So there are 3 inches of room on each side of the name.

173. Library Books Overdue

174. 1 yard is .91 meters. Here's how to solve this. Since 1 inch = 2.54 centimeters and 36 inches = 1 yard, $36 \times 2.54 = 91.44$ centimeters. But 100 centimeters = 1 meter so divide 91.44 centimeters by 100 and you have .9144 or, rounded off, .91 meters.

175. a. A gross is a dozen dozen, or 144.

   b. If you give birth to sextuplets, you've given birth to six children.

   c. A fortnight is 14 days.

   d. There are five musicians in a quintet.

   e. "Kilo" means 1,000.

176. The total is 4,408.

   2000 lbs (one ton) $\times$ 4 (sides of a square) = 8000

   8000 $\div$ 2 (pints in a quart) = 4000

   4000 + 33 = 4033

   4033 + 366 (days in a leap year) = 4399

   12 – 3 = 9

   4399 + 9 = 4408

177. A 12-ft. flagpole's shadow would be 3 ft. If the 20-ft. flagpole casts a shadow of 5 ft., the shadow is $\frac{1}{4}$ of the flagpole's height $\left(\frac{5}{20}=\frac{1}{4}\right)$. So the 12-ft. pole's shadow would be $\frac{1}{4}$ its height. $12 \times \frac{1}{4} = 3$.

178. The time on clock F should be 8:55 (answer c). The time moves ahead by 50 minutes in each picture.

179. The boys should be able to mow the small strip of 900 sq. ft. in $\frac{1}{3}$ hour, or 20 minutes. A lawn that is 900 sq. yds. could be 30 yds. by 30 yds., or 90 ft. by 90 ft. $90 \times 90 = 8100$ sq. ft. 900 sq. ft. is $\frac{1}{9}$ of 8100 sq. ft., so the time it takes to mow the sm aller strip should be $\frac{1}{9}$ of 3 hours. $\frac{1}{9} \times 3 = \frac{1}{3}$ hour. $\frac{1}{3}$ hour is 20 minutes.

180. He will need 9 total shirts. He will need an 8th shirt clean when he takes the 7 dirty shirts to the cleaners on Monday. He'll need a 9th shirt to pick up his 7 clean shirts on Tuesday. Then he can start the cycle all over again on Wednesday.

Part III. Mathematical Reasoning

Visual

181. There are 10 maximum lines. Here is one way to do it:

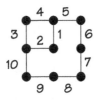

182. The mouse will exit at letter "G."

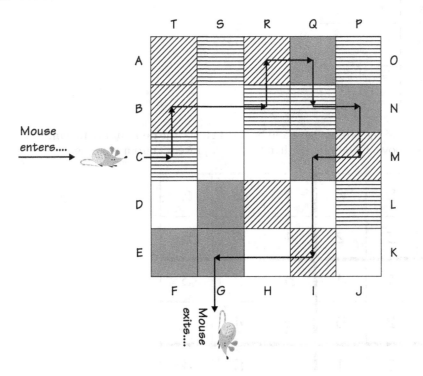

183. It takes two moves:

1. Move one Frisbee from stack #2 and place it on stack #3.

2. Move three Frisbees off stack #1 and set them in a stack by themselves. You now have four stacks of three Frisbees each.

184. Red, brown, green, blue, pink. From the first clue, the fifth piece of candy must be either blue or pink. From the third clue, blue is not last, so pink is. The green candy must be either second or third because it is between brown and blue. The red candy is next to the brown candy, and not fourth, so it can be only the first piece of candy, followed by brown, green, blue, and pink.

185. Place the bottom coin on top of the middle coin!

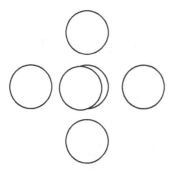

186. Here's where you should place your X.

X	O	X
→ X		O

or

→ X		O

Placing an X in the bottom left-hand box will give X the opportunity to win. Placing an X in the box above the bottom left-hand box will prevent O from winning.

187.

4	5	6	1	3	2
1	3	2	4	6	5
6	1	4	5	2	3
3	2	5	6	4	1
2	6	1	3	5	4
5	4	3	2	1	6

188. School Crosswalk

189. Illustration C cannot be created with one continuous stroke of the pen.

190.

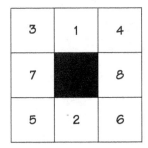

191. Here's one possibility, whose mirror image would work as well. Can you find other answers?

3	1	4
7	■	8
5	2	6

192. Remove toothpicks B and C and slide A down to where C was.

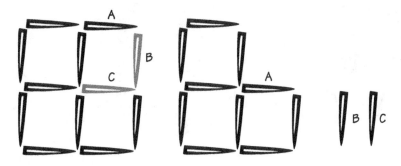

Did you find another way?

193. The maximum number of triangles you can make with two triangles is 8.

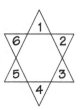

6 Small Triangles
2 Large Triangles
—————————
8 Total Triangles

194. Here's one way. But there are other ways with different shaped triangles. Can you find them?

195. Move coin #1 as shown below:

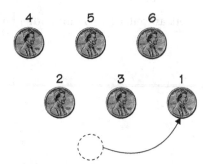

Now move coin #4 above and between coins #5 and #6.

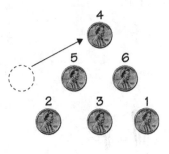

OR

Simply drop coins #4 and #6 straight down.

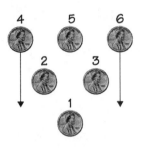

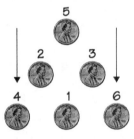

196. Staying After School

197. Here's what the decoded secret message says:

PUZZLES ARE FUN TO SOLVE!

The alphabet shift looks like this:

A B C D E F G H I J K L M N O P Q R S T U V W X Y Z

D E F G H I J K L M N O P Q R S T U V W X Y Z A B C

198. The least number of moves would be four. Yes, it is possible to visit all eight cubes.

Enter at ①, go up 90° to ②, turn 90° to ③, and turn 90° to the back cube for ④.

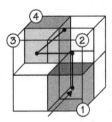

199. Illustration F is different. The tails on the end are both pointing to the middle of the illustration. Only one tail is pointing inward on the other illustrations.

200. There are eight ways. Here are the combinations:

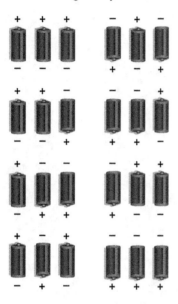

201. You can create seven sections from the intersections of three circles of the same size.

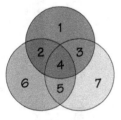

202. Yes. There are two more ways:

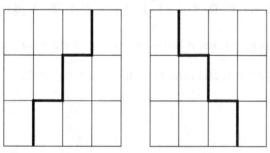

203. There are several ways to do this, but one of the easiest and quickest ways is to cut each brownie diagonally, and each of the four kids can eat three pieces.

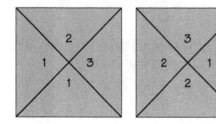

Can you find other ways?

204. Stop Messing Around

205.

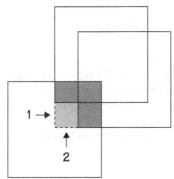

206.

7		4		3		8		2
9	8	5		0		1	3	4
7	0	■	5	9	4	■	2	9
3	0	8	9	■	8	5	4	5
	7	2	6	6	9	0	1	
1	0	3	1	■	5	2	0	6
5	8	■	7	7	8	■	3	2
2	4	1		5		6	0	0
1		6		6		3		7

207. There are eleven squares in the illustration—one large square forming the outside, four smaller squares each sharing a corner with the larger square, one medium-size square in the center of the illustration, two smaller squares within that middle square, and three even smaller squares within that middle square.

208. Illustration B is the odd one out. It is the only illustration with three sides or pieces. The others all have four.

209.

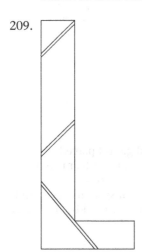

210. An octagon has 20 diagonals. Here is a chart of how the number of diagonals increases with each figure:

Square—2	Heptagon—14	Decagon—35
Pentagon—5	Octagon—20	Hendecagon—44
Hexagon—9	Nonogon—27	Dodecagon—54

How many diagonals would a dodecagon have? A dodecagon has 12 sides—54 diagonals. The formula for finding the number of diagonals for any polygon is number of diagonals = $n(n - 3)/2$ . . . where "n" is the number of sides of the polygon.

211. With five teams there would be a total of ten games. The schedule would look something like this:

For three teams there would be three games:

$$1\text{-}2 \quad 2\text{-}3$$
$$1\text{-}3$$

For four teams there would be six games:

$$1\text{-}2 \quad 2\text{-}3 \quad 3\text{-}4$$
$$1\text{-}3 \quad 2\text{-}4$$
$$1\text{-}4$$

Here's a chart showing the relationship between the number of teams and the total games played:

Teams	Total Games
3	3
4	6
5	10
6	15
7	21

Notice the relationship between the number of teams and the total games played. For each additional team, the total number of games will be the number of teams plus the total number of games. *Example:* Four teams will play six games; 4 + 6 = 10, and 10 is the total number of games that would be played by five teams; six teams would play 15 games, 6 + 15 = 21, and 21 is the total number of games that would be played by seven teams; etc. For eight teams, there would be 28 total games.

Part III

212. The club will need five sheets of paper.

Note: Sheet number 5 is the largest square, and the other squares fit over it.

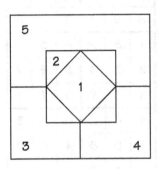

213. Here is the series of jumps to end up with only one penny:

7 to 9

2 to 7

10 to 8

7 to 9

3 to 8

8 to 10

10 to 3

1 to 6

Is there another way to end up with only one penny?

214. Cut the cake in half. Now cut in fourths.

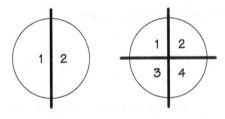

Now cut it in half sideways.

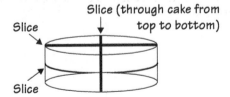

215.

5	1	2	4	3	9	7	6	8
6	8	4	5	7	1	9	2	3
3	7	9	2	8	6	4	5	1
4	3	5	6	9	8	1	7	2
8	6	7	1	5	2	3	9	4
2	9	1	3	4	7	6	8	5
1	2	8	7	6	4	5	3	9
9	5	6	8	1	3	2	4	7
7	4	3	9	2	5	8	1	6

#1

9	7	1	8	2	5	3	4	6
8	2	6	4	7	3	1	5	9
3	5	4	6	9	1	2	7	8
7	6	2	1	8	9	5	3	4
1	9	5	2	3	4	8	6	7
4	3	8	5	6	7	9	2	1
5	8	7	9	4	2	6	1	3
6	1	3	7	5	8	4	9	2
2	4	9	3	1	6	7	8	5

#2

9	3	6	4	1	7	8	5	2
8	7	2	3	5	6	1	9	4
5	4	1	2	9	8	7	3	6
2	8	7	9	6	1	3	4	5
4	1	9	5	2	3	6	8	7
6	5	3	8	7	4	9	2	1
1	9	5	6	3	2	4	7	8
3	6	8	7	4	5	2	1	9
7	2	4	1	8	9	5	6	3

#3

8	6	5	9	2	1	4	3	7
9	3	4	7	5	8	6	2	1
1	7	2	4	3	6	9	5	8
2	4	1	3	8	9	7	6	5
6	5	9	2	7	4	1	8	3
7	8	3	6	1	5	2	4	9
3	1	6	8	4	7	5	9	2
4	2	7	5	9	3	8	1	6
5	9	8	1	6	2	3	7	4

#4

216. The missing letter is R. The phrase spells out "Can you find this answer?"

CANY OUFI NDTH ISAN SWER?

217. Connect the Dots

218. It is better to go second. In fact, regardless of how many pennies the first player takes, you can always win by making the correct move in the second position.

219. The letter R. Working backward, the letter above K is F. Three letters to the right of F is I. Two letters below I is S. And the letter left of S is R.

220.

Start

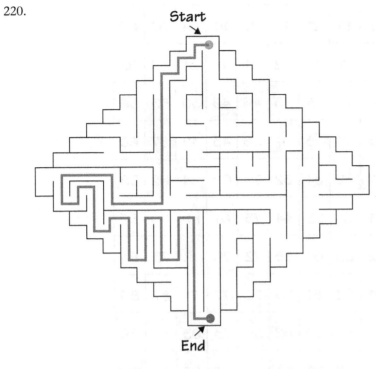

End

Start

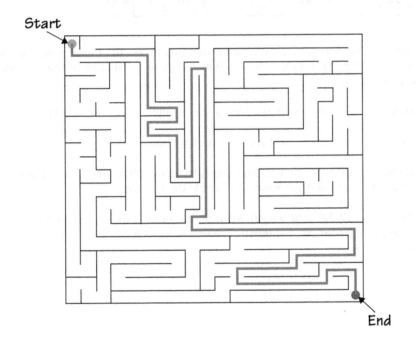

End

221.

1	6	9	12	19	21	17	12	10	54	57	60
10	4	5	14	17	30	32	41	8	51	49	52
13	6	2	16	14	15	43	46	49	50	53	56
17	19	12	18	17	35	37	36	43	42	57	60
15	21	23	27	32	34	32	70	68	64	62	59
28	26	22	21	31	33	44	73	67	69	60	57
31	25	24	32	63	67	65	72	75	72	73	84
35	42	43	61	62	61	78	79	77	71	82	80
32	45	41	58	86	83	82	80	78	93	97	99
41	49	52	56	87	79	84	87	89	90	88	100

222. a. 123. Adding the first two numbers on the bottom line makes the number on the line above them. The pyramid is built from the bottom up, so the missing number is the sum of the row below.

b. 9T. The numbers are counting up; the letters are the alphabet in reverse order.

c. 24. First add five, then for the next number, subtract one.

d. 9. Add the two numbers on the bottom of each triangle, subtract that from the number on top of each triangle, and put what's left inside the triangle.

223. The streets are not really the same length. Main St. has more hills that are steeper, so Michelle has to travel farther up and down. The overhead view from the airplane would not show hills.

224.

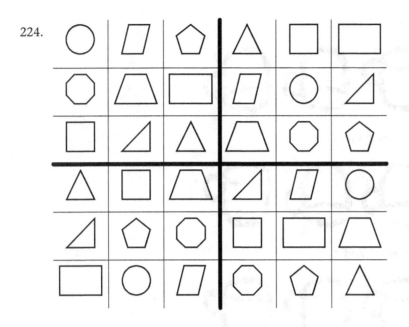

225. Cale can take 10 different routes with six squares.

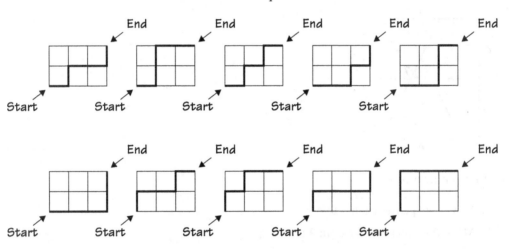

226. a. **9**, starting with 2, turn each number clockwise one-quarter turn.

b. **℮**, starting with the number 1, every other number is a mirror image.

c. , in order, these pairs of numbers total 10, with 1, 2, 3, 4, 5 being larger than their matching numbers 9, 8, 7, 6, 5, respectively.

227. Move #1:   Move cups 1 and 3.

Move #2:   Move cups 2 and 4.

Move #3:   Move cups 2 and 3.

228.

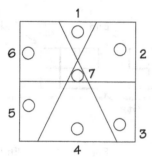

229. It takes nine moves:

1. Move the quarter from 5 to 4.

2. Move the other quarter from 2 to 5.

3. Move the penny from 1 to 2.

4. Move the quarter from 5 to 6.

5. Move the penny from 2 to 5.

6. Move the nickel from 3 to 2.

7. Move the nickel from 2 to 1.

8. Move the penny from 5 to 2.

9. Move the penny from 2 to 3.

Can you find another way?

230. Circle the Bases

Part III

231. a. Yes

b. No

c. Yes

d. No

232.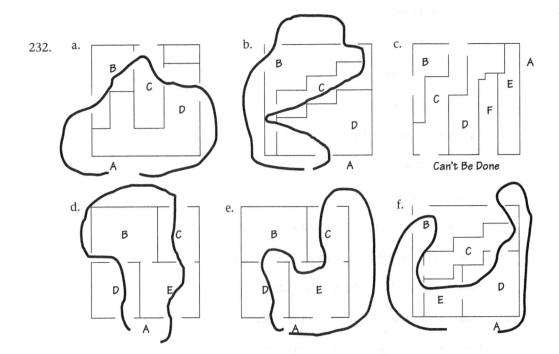
c. Can't Be Done

233. Here's one way. Did you find another?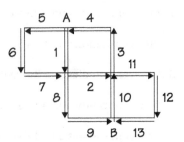

Other

234. All the capital letters shown will look the same if you hold them up to a mirror.

235. R is the next letter, and it's the last letter that can be used. These are the capital letters in which all or a portion of their design is closed.

236. The side opposite the side with four dots has three dots. Pivot the first die to the left so the two dots are to the right; it will be in the same position as the second die. Therefore, you can see that the five dots are opposite the side with two dots, for a total of seven (5 + 2). Since all opposite sides have the same sum, there must be three dots opposite the four dots to also equal seven.

237. d. There are 19 different amounts to be made.

    1. 1 three-cent candy = 3¢

    2. 2 three-cent candies = 6¢

    3. 3 three-cent candies = 9¢

    4. 1 five-cent candy = 5¢

    5. 2 five-cent candies = 10¢

    6. 3 five-cent candies = 15¢

    7. 4 five-cent candies = 20¢

    8. 1 three-cent candy and 1 five-cent candy = 8¢

    9. 2 three-cent candies and 1 five-cent candy = 11¢

   10. 3 three-cent candies and 1 five-cent candy = 14¢

   11. 1 three-cent candy and 2 five-cent candies = 13¢

   12. 2 three-cent candies and 2 five-cent candies = 16¢

   13. 3 three-cent candies and 2 five-cent candies = 19¢

   14. 1 three-cent candy and 3 five-cent candies = 18¢

   15. 2 three-cent candies and 3 five-cent candies = 21¢

   16. 3 three-cent candies and 3 five-cent candies = 24¢

   17. 1 three-cent candy and 4 five-cent candies = 23¢

   18. 2 three-cent candies and 4 five-cent candies = 26¢

   19. 3 three-cent candies and 4 five-cent candies = 29¢

238. Molly's last name is Reilly, and Maggie's last name is Ryan. You know that one of the first two statements must be true because Molly has to have one of those two last names. That means the third statement is false, since two of the three statements are false. Because it is false, Maggie's last name is Ryan, and Molly's last name is Reilly.

239. Courtney ate two slices.

Emma ate three slices.

Thomas ate seven slices.

Kevin ate eight slices.

240. PUZZLES ARE A HOOT!

To decode this message, simply match the number to the corresponding letter in the alphabet.

A B C D E F G H I J K L M N O P Q R S T U V W X Y Z
1 2 3 4 5 6 7 8 9 10 11 12 13 14 15 16 17 18 19 20 21 22 23 24 25 26

241. False. Just because Bob has a bat doesn't qualify him as a baseball player. He may have received it as a present but never used it.

242. 50-Yard Dash

243. Marcie can make 18 different outfits. Each shirt can be matched with each pair of shorts:

T-Shirt 1 — Shorts 1 / Shorts 2 / Shorts 3

T-Shirt 2 — Shorts 1 / Shorts 2 / Shorts 3

T-Shirt 3 — Shorts 1 / Shorts 2 / Shorts 3

That's 9 different combinations. Since each outfit can have either one of two different sandals, that's 9 × 2, or 18 different outfits. Notice that 3 × 3 × 2 = 18.

244. Here's one way to solve this:

POST

PAST

CAST

CART

CARE

245. Brad

Sharon

Sally

Barb

Brad is taller than Barb and Sharon, as can be seen from the first two statements. So Brad is either the tallest or second tallest. Sharon is taller than Sally, and since Sally is *not* the shortest, Sharon must be the tallest or second tallest, which means that Sally is third and Barb is the shortest. Since Brad can't be next to Sally, then Sharon must be. Sharon is the second tallest, leaving Brad to be the tallest.

246. Eighty comes before seventy, forty, fifty, and sixty in the dictionary!

247. The next letter is M. These are the first letters of the days of the week starting with Sunday and going backward in the week.

<u>S</u>unday

<u>S</u>aturday

<u>F</u>riday

<u>T</u>hursday

<u>W</u>ednesday

<u>T</u>uesday

<u>M</u>onday

248.

```
 T H I R T E E N █ █ █ █ M █ D
 I █ █ █ R █ S U R F A C E █ S
 M █ G R I D █ █ I █ G █ █ S
 E █ E █ █ P O L Y G O N █ █ C
 S L O P E █ E L █ O H E █ █ A
 █ █ M █ X █ L A █ G T U T O R
 A █ E █ P E N C I L █ S █ █ E
 R A T I O █ E █ C █ D █ █ E
 E █ R █ N █ █ E █ M I N U S
 A N Y █ E Q U A L S █ A █ █
 █ █ █ █ N █ █ R █ E █ G █ P
 L E S S T H A N █ R O O T █ O
 I █ U █ █ █ X █ █ I █ N █ I
 N █ M █ █ █ I █ H E X A G O N
 E █ █ P L U S █ █ S █ L █ █ T
```

249. WA. These are part of an alphabetical listing of two-letter state designations used for mailing and with ZIP Codes.

   RI = Rhode Island

   SC = South Carolina

   SD = South Dakota

   TN = Tennessee

   TX = Texas

   VI = U.S. Virgin Islands

   UT = Utah

   VT = Vermont

   VA = Virginia

   WA = Washington

250. You're back on the 8th floor, where you started! This is a good puzzle to start with the answer and work your way back. You were let out at the 8th floor. You had come directly from the 6th floor because you were let out on the 8th floor after moving up 2 floors. Before the 6th floor, you had been down 3 floors, which would be 6 – 3, or the 3rd floor. Before that, you had been up 5 floors: 5 + 3 is the 8th floor—right where you started!

251. The scores were:

Khalid = 99

Ben = 97

Mindy = 95

Tess = 94

Hector = 91

1. Since Ben, Tess, and Mindy did not get the highest score and Mindy scored higher than Hector, Khalid had the highest score, 99.

2. We know that Tess received a 94.

3. If Ben scored higher than most (clue #4), he had to be second and outscore three others. So Ben had a 97.

4. From clue #3, we know that Mindy scored higher than Hector and Tess. Tess was the fourth highest score, so Hector must have had the 91.

	99	97	95	94	91
Mindy	X	X	O	X	X
Tess	X	X	X	O	X
Ben	X	O	X	X	X
Hector	X	X	X	X	O
Khalid	O	X	X	X	X

252. c. Daughter. (Use real-life examples and apply the family members to the question. It makes the question much easier.)

253. c. X. These are the capital letters that rest on two points.

254. Foreign Languages

255. ANTS

In each example, take the middle two letters of the first word and the last two letters of the last word to form the new word in parentheses.

CANE (ANTS) BATS

256. There were five goats and five people. Since there were the same number of humans and goats, you can treat the puzzle as if one unit of people/goats had six legs: 30 ÷ 6 is 5. Try it with 60 legs: 60 ÷ 6 is 10, so there would be 10 goats and 10 humans.

257. a. 5. Washington is on the one-dollar bill; Lincoln is on the five-dollar bill.

b. $1.00

c. Jefferson. Lincoln is on the penny; Jefferson is on the nickel.

d. $1,000. $1 is to $100 as $10 is to $1,000. $100 \times 10 = 1,000$

258. K K Q Q K

259. a. so frantic

b. mild canoe tip

c. a clean guest

d. he owns lumber

e. a metric hit

260. a. Since there are six dots and each one can be blank or raised on any character, there would be $2 \times 2 \times 2 \times 2 \times 2 \times 2$, or 64 possible combinations.

b. This is the letter "X"

The sequence is every fourth letter → A, D, H, L, P, X.

261. a.
5 0

b.
1 0 0

c.
2 0 0 7

d. $= 48$ The equation is $\frac{24}{48} = \frac{1}{2}$

262. a. ▬ ▬ ▬ ▬ ▬ is the Morse code representation for a comma.

b. ▬ ▬ ▬ ▬   ▬ ▬ ▬ ▬   ▬ ▬ ▬ ▬ (The shaded section is a "slash /" character used for fractions and division.)

c. Puzzles are fun!

d. $\dfrac{\text{▬ ▬ ▬ ▬}}{\text{▬ ▬ ▬ ▬}} = \dfrac{3}{6} = \dfrac{8}{16} = \dfrac{1}{2}$

Now try to create your own code by using new symbols and combining them with both Braille and Morse code. For example, you could create a code in which every other letter is a different system: the first letter is Morse code, the second letter is Braille, the third letter is Morse code, etc.

263. The father has four sons and three daughters.

264. Check Your Answer

265. There are 15 total handshakes.

5 handshakes here ⟶	1–2	1–4	1–6
	1–3	1–5	
4 handshakes here ⟶	2–3	2–5	
	2–4	2–6	
3 handshakes here ⟶	3–4	3–6	
	3–5		
2 handshakes here ⟶	4–5		
	4–6		
1 handshake here ⟶	5–6		

266. There are 13 ways. Here they are in order of who comes first:

1. All three tie

2. Millie, Molly, Mookie

3. Millie, Mookie, Molly

4. Molly, Mookie, Millie

5. Molly, Millie, Mookie

6. Mookie, Millie, Molly

7. Mookie, Molly, Millie

If two of the girls tie:

8. Molly, (Millie and Mookie tie for second)

9. Mookie, (Millie and Molly tie for second)

10. Millie, (Mookie and Molly tie for second)

11. (Molly and Millie tie for first), Mookie

12. (Mookie and Millie tie for first), Molly

13. (Molly and Mookie tie for first), Millie

267. ALLIGATORS ARE ORNERY BECAUSE THEY GOT ALL THEM TEETH AND NO TOOTHBRUSH. — THE WATERBOY

268. Each word is scrambled.

FROM THERE TO HERE, AND HERE TO THERE, FUNNY THINGS ARE EVERYWHERE. — DR. SEUSS

269. There are eight letters in "this note."

270. Ms. Center must play forward because the person who responded to her plays guard (and Ms. Center cannot play the position of center). This means that the person who plays guard must be Ms. Forward and Ms. Guard must play the forward position.

271. Brenda is 12, Larry is 11, Lucy is 10, and Joe is 9.

272. e. Colts Bite Once

273. She takes the Boa alone to the new area, leaving the King Cobra and the Anaconda. She then comes back and brings King Cobra to the new quarters but brings back the Boa. She leaves the Boa and brings the Anaconda to the new quarters. So now the King Cobra and the Anaconda are in the new quarters. She now goes back to move the Boa from the old area to the new quarters.

274. c. The storm they heard about was moving faster than 60 miles per hour.

275. a. Each word has "cal" in it.

b. Each word begins and ends with the same three letters.

c. Each word has a vowel (or consonant) for every other letter.

d. Each word has three consecutive letters of the alphabet.

e. Each word has three O's.

276. Reggie was a baseball player who had singled, stolen second, and then had a collision with the catcher at home. He was out, by the way.

277. If you throw a ball into the air. The faster it goes up, the longer it will take to come back down. A second example would be playing tennis. The harder you hit a high lob shot, the longer it will take to reach your opponent.

278. Order Online

279. Claudia Marcos lived in ancient Rome and was 32 years old in 1723 B.C. Five years later would have been 1718 B.C., and she would have been 37.

280. Everyone trades bikes after they are assigned. Remember—it's the *bike* that finishes last that is the winner. If everyone trades bikes, they all will try to go as fast as they can so the bike originally assigned to them finishes last.

281. In the dictionary

282. They already are facing each other.

283. This time he was driving the right direction all right—he was just driving backward.

284. The professor was killed by his friend Shelley—whom he called Shell, for short. He had just enough time before he died to put the number 11345 on his calculator—which spells "SHELL" upside down.

285. The puzzle refers to the letters associated with each number on a telephone keypad.

   a. HELP: 4357

   b. SCHOOL: 724665

   c. PUPPY: 78779

286. A nightingale

$$G=1, A=2, L=3, H=4, N=5, T=6, I=7, E=8$$

287. Howie asks the boy, "Which way is your town?" If the boy is from Liarsville, he will point to Truism because he has to lie. If he is from Truism, he will point to Truism because he always tells the truth. Either way, he will point to Truism.

Part IV. Algebra, Statistics, and Probability

288. France won 9 bronze medals and 9 silver medals. Since Spain and the United States won 18 of the 20 gold medals, France must have won the remaining 2 gold medals. There are 60 medals in all, and one-third of that is 20 medals. 20 – 2 leaves 18 medals of combined bronze and silver for France. Since they won an equal number of each, that means they won 9 silver and 9 bronze medals.

289. Penny: $2x + 2y = 16$

   Brenda: $3x + y = 14$

   Molly: $x + y = 8$

   $x = 8 - y$

   Substitute this value back into the equation for Brenda's equation of $3x + y = 14$ and you get $3(8 - y) + y = 14$. You could have substituted $x = 8 - y$ into Penny's equation, as well.

$$24 - 3y + y = 14$$

$$\text{So, } -2y = -10$$

$$y = 5$$

$$x = 3$$

290. d. Either C or D has to be positive.

291. Here's what Marla wrote.

   First she set up a legend of what she knew:

   Marla had x pieces of candy.

   Ron had $3x$ pieces.

   If Ron gave her 7 pieces, she would then have $x + 7$ and he would then have $3x - 7$. But she now knows that they have an equal number, so she set both expressions equal to each other:

$$x + 7 = 3x - 7$$

   Move the unknowns to one side and the numbers to the other side:

$$2x = 14$$

$$x = 7$$

   So Marla started with 7 pieces and Ron had three times that, or 21.

292. The three page numbers were 114, 115, and 116. Here's how Rene's mom approached this. First she set up a legend:

x = the first of the three pages

$x + 1$ = the second of the three pages

$x + 2$ = the third of the three pages

$$x + (x + 1) + (x + 2) = 345$$
$$3x + 3 = 345$$
$$3x = 342$$
$$x = 114, \text{ which is the first page}$$
$$x + 1 = 115$$
$$x + 2 = 116$$

293. Seven Periods in a School Day

294. A = 4
B = 2
C = 8

```
  42
 +42
 ____
  84
```

Notice that B + B = A. This means that B must be one-half of A. Since we are working with positive numbers only, that means B must be 2 and A is 4. If B were 4, then A would have to be 8 and you would have a three-digit total. We have the total of CA, or 84.

295.
```
4  2  6
      5
      7
8  3  1        A and B are interchangeable.
```

A=4

B=2

C=6

D=5

E=7

F=8

G=3

H=1

296. The two numbers are 40 and 120.

$$x = \text{the smaller number}$$

$$3x = \text{the larger number}$$

$$3x + x = 160$$

$$4x = 160$$

$$x = 40$$

$$3x = 120 \text{ — more ice cream, please.}$$

297. Let's say Tilly has x number of hits. Since she's been up to bat 200 times and has a .425 average, we can set up this equation:

$$\frac{x}{200} = \frac{425}{1000}$$

Cross-multiplying will give you $1000x = 425$ times 200 or 85,000. Dividing each side of the equation by 1,000, we get $x = 85$. Tilly has 85 hits so far for the year.

298. The average of all her math grades is 94. If Linda had three 93's, she had 3×93, or 279 total points for those three tests. Likewise, she had 96×4, or 384 points total on the geometry tests and 89 total points on the last test. $279 + 384 + 89 = 752$ points over 8 tests ($3 + 4 + 1 = 8$), so her overall math average is 752 points divided by 8, or 94.

299. The answer is $\dfrac{5\frac{1}{7}}{12}$. There are several ways to do this, but one of the easiest and most effective ways is to set up a proportion like this:

$\dfrac{3}{7} = \dfrac{x}{12}$ and solve for x. If you know that the product of the means is equal to the product of the extremes, you can cross-multiply to solve for x.

$$\frac{3}{7} = \frac{x}{12}$$

$$7x = 36$$

$$x = \frac{5\frac{1}{7}}{12}$$

300. 4 days after the first day, for a total of 5 days. Let $x + 1 =$ the total number of laps Regina will run, realizing that x will be the number of days in the future that both girls will run for her sister to have twice as many laps. Rellie will run the same number of days (x), but she has 6 more laps to begin and her total laps will be twice her sister's. If you multiply Regina's total of ($x + 1$) by 2, it will equal Rellie's ($x + 6$).

$$2(x + 1) = (x + 6)$$

$$2x + 2 = (x + 6)$$

$$x = 4 \text{ days}$$

301. a. 4 hours

   b. 240 miles

   c. Since the trip took 4 hours and they covered 240 miles, they averaged $\frac{240}{4}$ or 60 miles per hour. Because the line is straight, Maria's father drove at 60 miles per hour for the entire trip.

302. $\frac{2}{3}$ or 2 in 3 chances. There are four possibilities for two children:

   BB   BG   GB   GG

   You already know that Margaret's uncle has one boy, so you can disregard GG. Now you have BB, BG, and GB. A girl appears in two of the three choices.

303. To be certain of getting 2 blue socks, the man would have to pull out 22 socks. Although unlikely, the man possibly could pull the 8 brown socks and 12 black socks first, which is a total of 20 socks. Then the next 2 he pulled would be blue.

304. Backpack

305. a. $\frac{2}{8}$ or $\frac{1}{4}$. Of the 8 sections, 2 are blue, so you have a 2 in 8, or 1 in 4 chance of spinning blue.

   b. 5 of 8. There are 3 red sections, so 8 – 3, or 5 of the 8 sections are not red.

   c. $\frac{4}{8}$ or $\frac{1}{2}$. There are 3 red sections and 1 green section, so 4 of the 8 sections are either red or green.

   d. $\frac{2}{3}$. There are $\frac{2}{8}$ chances of landing on blue and $\frac{3}{8}$ chances of landing on red:

   $$\frac{2}{8} \div \frac{3}{8} = \frac{2}{3}$$

306. Four quarters. Even if Dinesha gets three different-colored gumballs on the first three quarters, the fourth gumball will match one of the first three colors.

   After she puts in four quarters, she will have at least two gumballs of the same color. Let's say she has two red, one blue, and one white. If she puts in a fifth quarter, she may get one more red gumball, but she also may get a blue or white gumball. The same is true with a sixth quarter. Then she may have two blues, two whites, and two reds. But the seventh quarter will result in three of one color for certain.

307. Since there are 2 days a week and 4 weeks in each month, Jamie's mom is making 8 desserts in 28 days, or 2 in 7 days, every month for 9 months. So the chances are 2 in 7 on any day during the school year. If you based the answer on the entire year, you would simply multiply $\frac{3}{4} \times \frac{2}{7} = \frac{6}{28} = \frac{3}{14}$. The reason you multiply by $\frac{3}{4}$ is

   9 months is $\frac{3}{4}$ of a year: $\frac{9 \text{ months}}{12 \text{ months}} = \frac{3}{4}$